PROJECT
GOVERNANCE

PROJECT
GOVERNANCE

A practical guide to effective project decision making

ROSS GARLAND

**KOGAN
PAGE**

London and Philadelphia

Publisher's note

Every possible effort has been made to ensure that the information contained in this book is accurate at the time of going to press, and the publishers and author cannot accept responsibility for any errors or omissions, however caused. No responsibility for loss or damage occasioned to any person acting, or refraining from action, as a result of the material in this publication can be accepted by the editor, the publisher or the author.

First published in Great Britain and the United States in 2009 by Kogan Page Limited

120 Pentonville Road	525 South 4th Street, #241
London N1 9JN	Philadelphia PA 19147
United Kingdom	USA
www.koganpage.com	

© Ross Garland, 2009

ISBN 978 0 7494 5306 0

British Library Cataloguing-in-Publication Data

A CIP record for this book is available from the British Library.

Library of Congress Cataloging-in-Publication Data

Garland, Ross.
  Project governance : a practical guide to effective project decision making / Ross Garland.
      p. cm
  Includes bibliographical references and index.
  ISBN 978–0–7494–5306–0
  1. Project management. I. Title.
  HD69.P75G38 2009
  658.4′04--dc22

                                                                    2008039200

Typeset by Saxon Graphics Ltd, Derby
Printed and bound in India by Replika Press Pvt Ltd

Dedicated to Dace and Isabella

Contents

Preface

Some years ago I was consulting to an organization that did not have the best track record in project delivery – projects were regularly running over budget and were invariably behind schedule. My work for them was not intended to address this issue but did necessitate an investigation of their project governance arrangements. Project governance is the framework within which project decisions are made. It incorporates the structures that are established along with the terms of reference of the various governance bodies and role statements indicating the accountabilities and responsibilities of those who work within the decision-making arrangements. It is an important factor in project delivery. My investigation uncovered a complex and largely unworkable set of relationships between various committees, boards and executives with no clear and logical project governance arrangements. Since the organization had a large and growing capital works programme and because project governance was already related to my existing work with the organization, I offered to investigate this area with a view to creating something workable.

The first step in this task was to determine what information and models on project governance were already in existence and from which we could borrow. What followed was a largely fruitless internet search revealing very little information that specifically addressed project governance. Certainly some work had been done in this area, most notably covered by the PRINCE2 project management methodology, but the information on project governance tended to be peripheral rather than a central focus. To adequately serve the client, I needed more than what was on offer. I wanted to understand the principles that underpinned good project governance, to know how the governance structure could address the needs of stakeholders, to know how to populate the governance structure so that the right people held the right positions that would ensure good project outcomes, and how to scale the project governance arrangements to meet the needs of projects with differing risk profiles. I also needed to understand how project governance related to the other elements within the project development space – key documents, milestones, estimates and so on.

> Project governance is the framework within which project decisions are made.

Since the answers I required weren't readily available, I set out to develop them, starting with first principles and drawing on my experiences and those of others gained on many projects over many years. Because this particular organization delivered projects across many different industry sectors, the aim was to develop a project governance framework that would meet the needs of projects across all these sectors. The framework developed has proved very successful and now, some years later, continues to be the central focus of the organization's project development process in largely unchanged form. Since then I have worked with other organizations, refining and adopting the project governance framework to suit their particular needs.

This book was written for two reasons. The first was that there appeared to be very little guidance on the topic of project governance. The second was that the framework it describes works, and continues to work in a number of large organizations. This latter point is important. This book isn't a theoretical text. It's a practitioner's guide aimed at assisting those involved in the development and delivery of projects. Because of its focus on practitioners, the framework it describes is not overly complex, since complexity would only make its adoption and implementation more difficult for organizations.

It would be nice to say that the organizations that have implemented this project governance framework now deliver their projects on time and to budget. Nice, but not always true. The successful delivery of projects, especially large and complex ones, requires any number of factors to be properly addressed and project governance is only one of them. However, what can be said is that through the use of this framework, these organizations are now much better positioned to make efficient and effective decisions that support the successful delivery of their projects.

Acknowledgements

I wish to thank Tracey O'Meara and Bob Bidwell for being a constant source of ideas and providing the necessary sanity checks along the way. I am also in debt to them and John Tsoukas for reviewing the manuscript and providing many helpful comments. Eddie Peters has been a great help, not only for the Main Roads case study but also for his support and advice at the coal face of implementation, and I thank him for it. The 1998 electricity sector case study would not have happened without the assistance of Peter Davies and would not have been nearly as useful without the critical input of Chris Howe. Thank you both.

If you would like to contact the author, you can do so via his website at www.rossgarland.com.

Introduction

The importance of project governance

Projects are vitally important to organizations because it is through the successful delivery of projects that they are able to deliver services. Hence an organization that struggles to deliver its projects will also struggle to deliver the level of service its customers demand.

Project governance – the process of project decision making and the framework, models or structures that are established to enable this – is recognized as a critical success factor for the delivery of projects. The UK Government's Office of Government Commerce (OGC), owners of the world's de facto standard for project management methodology, PRINCE2 (OGC, 2005a) as well as the OGC Gateway™ Process have compiled a list of the eight common causes of project failure (OGC, 2005b). The list has been developed from over 1,000 reviews of high-risk UK Government projects since 2000. It refers to problems such as 'Lack of clear senior management... ownership and leadership' along with 'Lack of effective engagement with stakeholders', both important facets of project governance. For ICT projects, 'decision-making failures' is listed as one of the top five causes of project failure (OGC, undated a). In Australia, the Victorian Treasury lists similar issues as being associated with the failure of projects (Department of Treasury and Finance, Victorian Government, 2007).

> Project governance is a critical success factor for the delivery of projects.

The message is clear. Poor project governance leads to project failure. On the other hand, effective project governance positions a project for success. Good project governance allows effective and efficient decision making – that is, the right people making optimum decisions that meet the needs of the project and its stakeholders and making those decisions in a timely manner.

A unified approach to project governance

Few will disagree about the importance of project governance. What appears to be contentious is what constitutes good project governance. Certainly there often appears to be little consistency between the many different approaches to project governance in evidence in different organizations. Even within a single organization the governance of similar projects may be addressed using very dissimilar project governance arrangements – different committees, reporting arrangements, roles and so on. This lack of commonality surely doesn't make sense. Logic suggests that there should be a sufficient degree of similarity in the decision-making needs of projects to warrant at least some degree of uniformity in their project governance frameworks.

Later in this book the concept of the project lifecycle, which is the generic route map that projects follow from start to completion, is explored. At a detailed level, of course, all projects follow a different route map. But when a more strategic perspective is taken, projects are, or should be, very similar. They all have a beginning and an end, they all should develop a business case that justifies their cost and risk, most have some form of procurement involved (even if it is an in-house procurement), and so on. When the project development process is analysed at this strategic level, it becomes apparent that the controls and key decision-making mechanisms are, from the business manager's perspective, quite similar. For instance, all projects should be subject to questioning along the lines of:

- Does it fit the strategy of the organization?
- Does it meet the needs of the organization?
- Does it offer value for money?
- Does it have a reasonable likelihood of success?

These types of questions are not technically based and are not specific to any particular business sector. While there may be technical questions to be resolved on any project and these may be escalated to project governance bodies, the project governance arrangements should not be technically based. Instead, they need to focus on the desired business outcomes. It is in this respect that all project governance arrangements have a common focus and allow a unified approach to the governance of projects across different sectors. It doesn't matter whether the organization is building a new CRM capability or a motorway, senior executives in the organization still need to be asking similar questions to those above. The challenge is to develop a project governance framework that enables these decisions to be made effectively and efficiently.

The developers of the PRINCE2 Project Management Methodology clearly believe a consistent approach to project governance is achievable, and propose a single governance arrangement that can be applied to most, if not every, project's governance structure. PRINCE2 establishes a project board whose members represent the three key stakeholders of a project – the owner, the user and the supplier. PRINCE2 has expanded from its original role of serving the needs of the UK Government to become the world's pre-eminent project management methodology. This suggests that the PRINCE2 project governance structure broadly meets the project governance needs of most projects and so constitutes a unified approach to project governance across different project types and sectors.

However, since PRINCE2 covers most aspects of project delivery, its coverage of project governance is a small part of a much larger picture and the amount of guidance that it therefore provides in this specific area is somewhat limited. This is what this book sets out to address.

A practitioner's guide

The project governance framework developed in this book is designed to meet the needs of practitioners – business managers with an involvement or interest in project decision making. It takes the reader through the logical steps required for the establishment of a project governance framework for either a project or for project delivery across an organization. Commencing with problems typical of ineffectual project governance, it develops a set of principles designed to overcome these problems and builds a framework based on these principles. The book explains how to populate the framework effectively, provides the accountabilities and responsibilities of the main roles and describes how to implement the project governance framework within the organization. Effective stakeholder management is fundamental to project success – just refer again to the common causes of project failure referenced above – and the book provides guidance on how stakeholders' needs can be addressed and integrated within the project governance arrangements. It also shows how the project governance framework can be part of an overall project development framework that applies a consistent approach to the delivery of projects across an organization.

The project governance framework that is developed reflects the needs of large and complex projects; however, it also address the issue of scalability. This ensures the framework can be applied to lower-risk projects and meet their needs without unnecessarily burdening them and whilst still adhering to the principles developed. This enables maximum flexibility and avoids slavish adherence to a single construct.

The effective implementation and adoption of a project governance framework requires a strong and robust understanding of both the principles and details involved to ensure an optimum outcome for the project or organization. Implementing a project governance framework is a challenge. Without a complete knowledge of the 'why' and the 'how', the need for the framework will not be clear, it will lack full support throughout the organization and its adoption will be patchy and possibly flawed. Also, if practitioners don't understand why things are being done in a certain way, they are constrained in their ability to flex the arrangements to suit their particular needs. This book ensures that practitioners have the necessary information and understanding to make project governance work for them.

Who should read this book

This book has been written primarily for executives in medium to large organizations with a business interest in a project. Since expenditure on capital programmes in many organizations often equals or outstrips the organization's operational and maintenance spending, executives in such organizations are very likely to be involved in project developments at some point. This likelihood has increased over recent years with the increase in project activity, driven by a number of factors including:

- organizations' increasing use of information and communications technology (ICT) platforms to transform the manner in which they do business;
- the recent increase in development activity in emerging economies, which is driving the construction of new infrastructure;
- the increase in capital expenditure across many sectors in the mature economies in response to infrastructure under-spend in past decades;
- the major increase in construction activity in the mining sector as a result of the resources boom, with knock-on effects in rail and ports infrastructure.

Executives' involvement in projects can be from many different perspectives. The project may support their business, it may have an impact on their business or they may have involvement in its planning or execution. In all these cases they are likely to have a role to play in the governance of the project and they need to understand what that role is and how they engage with the project. The focus of this book is on the business and those business managers whose involvement in any particular project is driven by a business need and from a business perspective. Having said that, project (and programme) managers will find the book very helpful because they need to operate within the governance structures described. This book will therefore be particularly useful to:

- business managers involved with project boards, steering committees or other project governance structures;
- business managers who are stakeholders in a project;
- project managers;
- programme managers;
- executives in corporate policy areas seeking to improve their organization's delivery of projects.

Structure

- Introduction
- Chapter 1: Causes and symptoms of ineffective project governance. To develop an efficient and effective project governance framework, it is necessary to understand the causes and symptoms of poor project governance. This chapter examines some of the most common features associated with ineffective project decision-making structures.
- Chapter 2: The principles of effective project governance. This chapter develops a set of principles designed to overcome the symptoms and causes discussed in chapter 1.
- Chapter 3: Building the project governance model. This chapter constructs the basic project governance model and ensures it is consistent with the principles of chapter 2.
- Chapter 4: Populating the project board. The project governance framework is only effective when the right persons fill the right posts. This chapter provides guidelines on identifying the person best placed to fill each role within the project board.
- Chapter 5: Scalability. While the project governance framework developed in Chapter 3 can be used on any project, it is specifically designed for high-risk projects. This chapter provides options for customizing the project governance framework to suit various circumstances and especially to meet the needs of lower-risk projects.
- Chapter 6: Implementing the project governance framework. This chapter discusses the challenges of implementing the project governance framework across an organization.
- Chapter 7: The governance relationship between programmes and projects. This chapter discusses the relationship between programme and project governance and how the two work together.
- Chapter 8: Towards an integrated project delivery framework. This chapter describes how a project delivery framework can be developed, incorporating such components as key documentation, approvals, staged gates, project cost estimates, etc.

The book contains case studies that help to illustrate the project governance framework. It also includes a number of appendices providing useful examples of the terms of reference of the various governance bodies and responsibility statements for the various positions within those bodies, as well as an example of a project governance policy.

1 Causes and symptoms of ineffective project governance

Ahead of proposing any new project governance arrangements it's necessary to have a clear understanding of the problem itself. This chapter therefore investigates the root causes of ineffective project governance and the subsequent problems that arise. The simplest definition of a successful project is one that delivers the required outcome within the defined constraints of time, cost and quality. If any of these constraining parameters are significantly exceeded or compromised, or if the desired outcome is not achieved, then the project has, to some extent at least, failed. It is difficult to determine the extent to which a project's governance can be said to be the cause of project failure; however, this chapter investigates project governance failings that will definitely be detrimental to the health of a project. In some cases the symptom will be the result of more than just ineffective project governance; however, in all cases problems with project governance will be a significant contributing factor.

Many of the causes of project governance problems are interrelated and the list is by no means exhaustive. It has been developed through interactions with many projects and with many organizations that are regularly delivering projects. Readers of this book will have experiences of their own to add – examples of problems that have arisen on projects that either immediately signify governance issues or do so upon subsequent reflection. In most cases it should be possible to recognize a link between the causes that you have identified and those listed below.

Despite the interrelationships, an attempt has been made to instil some structure into this assessment through a loose categorization of the fundamental causes of project governance related problems. The categories chosen are:

- confusion regarding the objectives of project governance;
- risk aversion;
- issues relating to organizational structure;
- stakeholder and ownership issues.

Once a better understanding of the causes of ineffective project governance is developed, criteria will be identified that any solution must meet in order to constitute an effective and efficient project governance framework.

Confusion regarding the objectives of project governance

Project governance is, or should be, established to fulfil one primary objective – to enable efficient and effective project decision making. The structure that is put in place to deliver this also has a number of side benefits. By its very nature a project governance structure supports project reporting and information dissemination and, to a degree, stakeholder management since key stakeholders are closely involved in the decision-making process. Project governance problems arise when these side benefits become the main driver for the project governance structure. When this occurs, there are a number of telltale signs.

An overemphasis on stakeholder management results in committees growing in size to cater for the full range of project stakeholders so that stakeholder management needs can more easily be accommodated. As committees grow in size, so their effectiveness as decision-making forums decreases.

A further issue is an overemphasis on reporting needs rather than effective decision making which often results in the project decision-making structure being integrated within the organization's structure. This arrangement results in committees reporting up through the line of command, which is helpful from a reporting perspective but which effectively negates the benefit of having a decision-making committee in the first place. A project governance structure is formed precisely because the organization's structure is not designed to meet the needs of project decision making. This blurring or integration of project structures and organization structures introduces a number of undesirable features:

- It adds multiple layers to the decision-making structure, which slows the decision-making process.
- Projects require timely decision making; serial decision making through the organizational hierarchy does not support this imperative.
- The organizational hierarchy includes persons in the decision-making process who may not be best placed to make project decisions. Whilst it may be safe to assume that officers within an organization are familiar with the day-to-day operations that they manage, the same knowledge cannot be assumed with respect to a complex project whose execution is very different from everyday operational activity, albeit a project that may have an impact on those officers' activities.
- It blurs accountability within the decision-making process since it becomes largely impossible to distinguish the different accountabilities of the different layers within the structure. In these situations, accountability normally defaults to the highest position in the decision-making chain. However, it may be that this role holder is not the best placed individual to make the key project decisions.

Another area that is sometimes intertwined with the project governance arrangements, resulting in confusion, is that of contract administration. There may be key decisions around the contractual arrangements that are rightfully dealt with within the project governance structure. However, generally speaking, the project governance structure should be dealing with delivery of the complete project as defined by the business case rather than the specific contractual arrangements between customer and supplier. If contract management becomes too enmeshed in the decision-making process, it detracts from the ability of decision makers to concentrate on the issues that define the project rather than the issues surrounding the contract.

Case study 1 at the end of this chapter (page 19) provides a good example of a project governance structure whose core objective of decision making has been diluted through confusion over what the structure is trying to achieve.

Risk aversion

There are many opportunities for an individual in an organization to reduce or 'smear' individual risk. Different organizations have different risk appetites and the risk culture of the organization is reflected in the approach of its officers. In large organizations, with their complex management structures and divisional arrangements, a risk-averse culture can become, to an extent, part of the fabric of the organization. This isn't always a bad thing – for some organizations, for instance a government treasury department, a healthy aversion to risk is a desirable attribute – but it can lead to unhealthy behaviour in the project governance environment. In large organizations there is always someone with whom an important decision can be checked or a superior that must it sign off. Decisions in one part of the organization will have an impact on other parts of the organization and so coordination and consultation requirements can easily reinforce risk averse cultures. Some of these approaches have become so institutionalized that it's unfair to point the finger at the individual since the method has itself become the accepted modus operandi of the organization.

These approaches reduce individual risk through joint or consensus decision making, where decisions involve numerous people across the organization. In this way the decision becomes shared. Clearly, this consensus approach to decision making is not without benefits. It does assist in achieving buy-in and it can help to ensure that the views of all key stakeholders are represented. This does not mean that it is the best means of achieving these outcomes, however, and the dis-benefits normally far outweigh the benefits. In particular, a consensus approach to decision making does not suit projects for four primary reasons:

- It is slow. In large organizations the consensus decision-making approach requires the decision to progress both up the chain of command and potentially, at each level, to progress across the divisional structure of the organization in an attempt to gain buy-in to the decision. This process is very time-consuming.

- The quality of the documentation that informs the decision can also suffer since managers in the chain can seek to justify their involvement through 'adding value' by making unwarranted or unhelpful changes. Each change sends the document in question back down the chain to start again. So potentially consensus decision making not only slows the decision-making process but adversely affects the quality of the outcome.
- This approach also means that those persons who are best placed to make project decisions have equal weighting or shared input with those with only peripheral involvement in the project or with a particular narrow perspective on the project. The outcome therefore is not necessarily 'best for the project' or the organization.
- The consensus-building approach blurs accountability. Accountability is a theme that is addressed often throughout this book and is the key to effective project governance. When consensus decision making is built into the project governance structure, the outcome can resemble that in case study 1. With a structure such as this it is not possible to have clearly defined roles because accountability cannot be sliced so finely between so many persons. Thus no one has a clear picture of their accountabilities or responsibilities, both of which are essential for clarity and speed of decision making.

A further means of reducing individual risk in an organization is to avoid making any decisions. This is achieved by continually gathering information and refining the solution – otherwise known as 'analysis paralysis'. Not only does the process itself intrinsically slow down the decision-making process, the underlying assumptions that the project is based upon can change in the time frames involved, thereby justifying more analysis and rework.

Issues relating to organizational structure

Organizational structures are primarily designed to facilitate the effective operation of a business on a day-to-day basis. The divisional nature of large organizations reflects this objective, as do the accountabilities established within the structure. Organizational accountabilities are arranged around the split of work between the various divisions in the organization and the management hierarchy.

Projects, on the other hand, are not driven by the need for routine or ongoing operational effectiveness and therefore have very different structural needs. Whereas the organization has ongoing operational needs as its primary focus and has an organizational structure designed to deliver this, the project is a very dynamic environment with a relatively short-term focus. Large projects create impacts across the organization. Their stakeholders are not neatly arranged within an organization chart but are scattered throughout it. It is therefore not surprising that the project's needs cannot be met by the existing organization structure.

This has a number of consequences for the project. It means the project cannot utilize the organizational structure for its own delivery purposes since that structure is not designed for delivering a project. It also means that the accountabilities of persons on the project, whatever they may be, cannot or should not borrow from the organization's accountabilities. This is because organizational accountabilities reflect the operational goals of the organization and these goals are different from those of the project; related, to be sure, but fundamentally different.

The organization sets out to overcome these problems through the establishment of a project committee, variously known as a project steering committee, project board or project control group. The intent is that key project stakeholders are brought together under the umbrella of, say, the steering committee to make decisions as a group, thereby ensuring stakeholder needs are met and the delays associated with serial or layered decision making are overcome. However, steering committees can quickly create their own problems.

As a general rule, when more than six persons are present in a decision-making forum, the benefit of gaining greater stakeholder involvement in the decision-making process starts to be overtaken by the inefficiencies associated with decision making in large groups. It is no secret that it is difficult for large committees to make effective and timely decisions. Steering committees often grow in size in an attempt to give voice to all parts of the organization affected by the project. As previously discussed, this addresses the inherent individual and organizational goals of creating consensus through consultation and also addresses the natural risk aversion present in many large organizations. It can also avoid the afore-mentioned problem of hierarchical or layered decision making. However, a large steering committee is not usually an effective decision-making body.

Steering committees also struggle with their relationship with the rest of the organization. This is particularly pertinent in respect of the authority that the steering committee holds and, therefore, the account-ability of those who sit on the steering committee. If the steering committee lacks the necessary authority then in effect it must become embedded in the organization structure such that decisions it makes can be ratified at a higher level. This of course negates one of the primary purposes of having a steering committee in the first place.

Project initiation

Large and complex projects can often take a long time to become fully established and recognized as a project entity within the organization. This process has been described as 'gaining traction' and if it is progressed inefficiently, the project can take much longer to deliver than would otherwise be the case. Gaining traction tends to revolve around the consensus-building process discussed above, as project stakeholders are gradually rallied to the project cause. While stakeholder buy-in is imperative, this is not an efficient means to achieve it.

This begs the question 'What constitutes the start of a project?' The generally accepted definition of a project is a temporary undertaking designed to deliver a one-off outcome or benefit. According to this definition, a project must have a start and a finish. The end of a project can be defined as when the process, system or asset is commissioned. But what constitutes the start? Is there any single point or activity that can be said to initiate a project? If an organization lacks clarity in their understanding of project initiation and what triggers it, how then can they efficiently deliver projects?

The answer is that all too often projects aren't effectively initiated and take an unnecessarily long time to establish themselves and gain the required 'traction' that enables them to progress. Quite often, the early project development process tends to be one of consensus building within the organization as officers at various levels build support for the project. Any consensus approach takes time and the more complex, costly and risky the project, the longer this approach takes.

The effective and efficient initiation of a project requires all concerned to understand and agree upon the initiation process. And there needs to be a single event that kick starts this process. This event occurs at the transition of the project from the organization structure to the project governance structure, at which point the accountability for the success of the project should be established. As soon as an executive is identified as being accountable for the project and is given the necessary authority, the project can be said to be initiated. Prior to this, progress is likely to be slow and haphazard since no one person has responsibility for project development. Thus any confusion between the organization structure and the project governance structure can have an impact on the speed with which the project gains traction. The project initiation process is discussed further on page 64.

The purchaser/provider model

The purchaser/provider arrangement is worthy of special mention in any discussion of project governance problems relating to the structure of the organization. In this model the organization recognizes that its business units can be associated with either of two core functions – a purchaser of services or a provider of services. The purchaser has an external service delivery focus and focuses on efficient delivery of services to its external customers. The assets it utilizes to provide these services require periodic upgrading or replacement in order to maintain the required level of service. Asset delivery is the remit of the provider side of the business. The provider is the repository of the organization's project management skills and focuses on the efficient delivery of assets to meet the needs of the purchaser. The arrangement is summarized in the box.

The purchaser/provider model

Purchaser

Focus:	service delivery
Primary skill set:	operational efficiency
Project role:	to identify the service delivery need and define the output specification for the provider

Provider

Focus:	asset delivery
Primary skill set:	project management
Project role:	deliver or procure delivery of the assets that meet the output specification

---

The purchaser/provider relationship is relatively common and present either explicitly or implicitly in many large organizations. While the theoretical concept that underpins this model is reasonable, it can also result in two related problems.

First, there is a tendency to interpret the purchaser/provider relationship as one in which the purchaser hands over responsibility for the delivery of the asset to the provider. On the face of it this seems to be in keeping with the basic premise of the model in that the asset delivery skill set resides within the provider and a handover is therefore logical. The issue here is that upon completion of the project, the purchaser has to operate it and integrate it within the spectrum of services the organization delivers. A handover with minimal further involvement until project completion runs the significant risk that what is delivered may not fully reflect the purchaser's needs, irrespective of the adequacy of the design brief or output specification delivered to the provider at the project's inception. As the project's business case gradually evolves from the early concept phase of the project towards a complete document that will inform the investment decision, there will be many decisions and issues requiring input from the purchaser that will serve to define the project. The greater the extent of the handover from purchaser to provider, the less the involvement of the former in these critical decisions.

In many respects, though, the concept of a handover can be very appealing. From the purchaser's perspective, not only do they save on the time and effort required to stay closely involved in the project, but also if the output is not to their satisfaction they have someone to blame. In this respect it is a wonderful way of seemingly offloading accountability onto the provider. The purchaser can seek to justify the handover with the argument that the project delivery skills lie within the provider's organization. Even then, the provider may not be unsupportive of this approach. If the provider has the ability to avoid or minimize the fallout resulting from the less-than-successful project that results, then it may view this arrangement as preferable to having to support and interact with the purchaser throughout the project's development. This is particularly the case if the purchaser lacks project delivery sophistication. Both parties therefore may have reasons for supporting the flawed argument that the purchaser/provider model implies a handover of accountability.

Second, and closely related to the 'handover' problem. is that of 'project capture' by the provider. In this scenario, the organization views the provider as the expert in all things project related. This mindset results in too much power and authority being vested in the provider – it results in the project becoming asset focused rather than service delivery focused. There are various indicators to this problem: the key decision-making forums may be chaired by the provider rather than the purchaser, there may be a lack of clarity around ownership of the business case, and, invariably, there is a lack of clarity around accountability on the project. This is discussed further in the next section.

There is nothing fundamentally wrong with the purchaser/provider model. It can work and is a logical means of organizing business units within an organization. For it to work, though, the accountabilities and responsibilities of each party in respect of projects need to be carefully considered and, in particular, must reflect the fact that projects deliver services rather than just assets.

Stakeholder and ownership issues

Key stakeholder support for a project is an essential ingredient for its success. Conversely, a lack of support by key stakeholders is likely to result in the project failing, remembering that those key stakeholders run business units whose cooperation is essential to project success. Whatever decision-making body is established for the project should itself comprise the central project stakeholders – not all stakeholders, since large committees seldom make effective decisions. However, the main stakeholders must be included in the decision-making forum. Projects run into problems when the decision-making forum does not contain the correct stakeholders and/or the project ownership is confused or split. This can result in disgruntled stakeholders and a lack of clarity around decision-making responsibility.

Ownership of a project is one of the main concepts that this book discusses. The most fundamental mistake that organizations make in establishing project governance structures is to misunderstand the concept of project ownership. What can happen is that the project is 'owned' or 'driven' or 'sponsored' or 'championed' by the group or individual with the responsibility for asset delivery rather than service delivery. Under such arrangements, ownership rests with the project management area and, as is discussed in the next chapter, this is not its rightful place.

Beyond project ownership, the broader question is how to determine which stakeholders should comprise the key decision-making forum and which should have their needs addressed through other stakeholder management mechanisms. The wrong answer potentially results in a failed project. Even if the project negotiates this potential pitfall, it faces the problem of how to address the needs of those stakeholders who are not part of the decision-making forum. If stakeholders don't have a seat on the decision-making forum, the project will certainly need to demonstrate that robust and effective mechanisms exist to address their needs.

Solution criteria

Not all of the above problems are solely the result of ineffectual project governance. Other factors contribute to these problems, including the skills, competencies and personalities of the people involved and the political environment in which the project operates. In so far as ineffective project governance is the cause of these problems, any project governance framework developed herein must address these problems and, as far as possible, resolve them. The extent to which the project governance framework can achieve this is one measure of its effectiveness.

The following is a summary of the problems discussed above, presented in terms of the issues that a project governance framework must address if it is to be effective.

- The project governance framework must be clear in its objectives. It must fundamentally address project decision making but must also address the structure that enables stakeholder management to be addressed.
- It must enable efficient and effective project decision making. In doing so, it must address issues such as multi-layered decision making resulting from organizational chain of command considerations as well as the tendency towards consensus decision making.
- It must provide clarity of accountability and clear and correct assignment of accountability.
- It must resolve the relationship between the organization's structure and the temporary structure put in place to deliver the project.

- It must support the project, delivering a service rather than being just an asset, since an asset is only a platform for delivering a service.
- It must ensure that the stakeholders who comprise the project's decision-making forum are those necessary to meet the needs of the project without including so many that its effectiveness is reduced.
- It must ensure that those stakeholders not included within the decision-making forum have their needs adequately met by the project governance framework.
- The project governance framework must support the efficient and effective initiation of projects.
- The project governance framework should support the effective operation of the purchaser/provider model.

The next step is to develop a set of principles that meet these criteria and that will form the basis of a project governance framework.

Executive summary: Causes and symptoms of ineffective project governance

Cause: Confusion regarding the objectives of project governance

The core objective should be efficient and effective project decision making. The core objective is *not*:

- stakeholder management (possible symptom: large and ineffective decision-making committees;
- project reporting (possible symptom: project governance structure embedded within organization structure);
- contract management (possible symptom: decision-making body has contract management focus).

Cause: Risk aversion

Possible symptoms include consensus decision making that involves many people across the organization, and analysis paralysis.

Cause: Issues relating to organizational structure

Possible symptoms include:

- large and ineffective decision-making committees;
- decision-making committees embedded within the organizational structure;
- a purchaser/provider model that is causing conflict.

Cause: Stakeholder and ownership issues

Possible symptoms include:

- disgruntled stakeholders;
- lack of clarity around decision-making responsibilities;
- confused project ownership;
- ownership residing with the project delivery group rather than the service delivery business unit.

Case study 1:
Ineffective project governance

Figure 1.1 shows the project governance structure established for a major infrastructure project undertaken a few years ago in Australia. Some of the details have been altered to preserve anonymity, though they are not material. This case study displays many of the problems associated with ineffective project governance.

The structure shown is a combination of many elements. It contains two boards, a working group, elements of a company's organizational structure, various agreements, contracts, a memorandum of understanding and so on. What role does such a structure play? It includes elements of decision-making structures, stakeholder management, information reporting and dissemination, and contract management. It cannot hope to achieve all of these things efficiently. Because of the lack

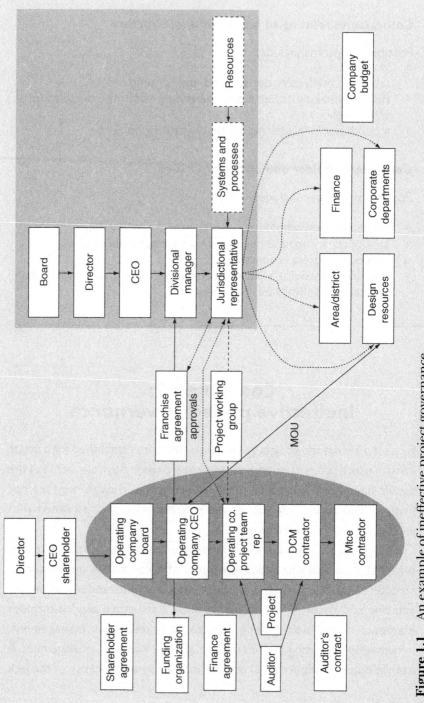

Figure 1.1 An example of ineffective project governance

of clarity regarding what it hopes to achieve, it creates confusion through its complex arrangements. A brief analysis reveals the following fundamental flaws in this structure:

- It is difficult to imagine there was any clear objective articulated for the development of this structure. Certainly there appears to be a blurring of project governance and organizational governance arrangements, with many elements of an organizational framework in evidence. In fact, strangely, what appears to be missing is one of the key elements of any project governance arrangement – a steering committee or project board.
- There is no clarity in this structure regarding individual or group responsibilities. There may be documentation that sits behind the diagram, but if so it is difficult to imagine that it provides a clear and unambiguous statement in this respect. Governance structures such as these are seldom accompanied by detailed role statements, primarily because the complexity of the structure overwhelms any attempt to provide such clarity.
- Accountability is blurred. In this respect it is little different to the issues around responsibilities of the various entities. It would be very difficult to ascribe clearly differentiated accountabilities to all the entities in the diagram. Overall accountability can only be presumed to rest at the top of the structure, but given there are two routes to the top even that doesn't resolve the confusion.
- It is unclear what decisions are made at any point in the structure. This is linked to the above issues of responsibility and accountability.
- The number of entities involved in the structure indicates significant confusion between the tasks of project decision making, stake-holder management and contract management. It is also suggestive of a consensus approach to decision making.

If anything, this structure appears to be a relationship diagram covering interfaces between the various project entities within the organization, including senior executives, contractors, stakeholders, the project team and project elements such as resources and finance. Without under-taking a detailed analysis it is not possible to determine the impact of this flawed governance structure on the project. However, at the time that this project was being developed, a separate project comparable in terms of size and complexity was also under development. The latter project used some elements of the project governance framework that are discussed in this book, although by no means all of them. That project reached financial close approximately two years ahead of the one illustrated in Figure 1.1. This is a significant difference in terms of both time and costs incurred by the project team. While not all this difference can be attributed to ineffectual project governance, there can be little doubt that the governance structure described in this case study does not support efficient and effective project decision making.

2 The principles of effective project governance

This chapter develops the principles of effective project governance. In doing so it reflects the solution criteria developed in the previous chapter, ensuring the principles solve the problems that were identified as resulting from ineffective project governance. The principles are then used as the basis of the design of the project governance model.

There is a further reason for developing a set of principles, which is closely linked to the fact that this book is written specifically for practitioners, from a practitioner's viewpoint. Irrespective of the fact that the project governance model developed later in this book is applicable to any project, there will invariably be factors or influences acting to prevent a clean and direct implementation of the model and necessitating the adoption of a compromise. In particular, personalities and politics will often play a part in the development of a project governance framework for any significant project. Under these circumstances the question becomes how far one can deviate from the model before the battle for effective project governance is lost. The answer lies in remaining consistent with the principles, which provide a broad framework in which to operate. Flexibility may require movement away from the model and in fact the book later addresses different ways of flexing the model to meet the particular needs of projects with different risk profiles. However, once one or more of the principles has been lost in the battle to accommodate the personalities and the politics influencing the project, the effectiveness of the resulting project governance framework will suffer.

The identification of the principles of effective project governance commences with a discussion on a concept that will be revisited many times in this book – accountability.

Accountability

If you work for a large organization, spare a few moments to think about a recent large project with which you were associated, perhaps even a current project. In your opinion, who was, or is, accountable for the success of that project? Was it the project manager or the project director? Perhaps it was the project sponsor or even the project steering committee? (Don't worry too much about terminology at this point.) If the project was particularly large, perhaps the view was accountability lay with the divisional manager or even the CEO. If government, perhaps it lay at ministerial level, or if in the private sector, at board level. Now ask yourself whether others in the organization would share your opinion. Would there be a common perspective on project accountability across the organization?

An exercise in accountability

I once ran a workshop for the executive team of a government organization that I suspected did not have an appreciation of the importance of project accountability. I took them through a very simple scenario where I described the governance arrangements of an imaginary large and high-risk project that they, as the project executive, had just been informed was well over budget and running significantly behind schedule – a scenario not uncommon in their experience.

I provided minimal information that nevertheless implied that the project manager was largely responsible for the dire situation the project found itself in and asked them who they held accountable for the failure of the project. Some duly nominated the project manager, while some nominated others. I then provided further information which suggested that the overruns were largely due to a major scope change demanded by the project director and that the project manager had acted correctly, and indeed had indicated to the project director the likely impact in terms of delivery time frames and project cost. I again asked them who they held accountable. With the situation now clearer and with more information to hand, many considered the project director to be accountable. And again there were a few non-conforming votes.

Then, I provided the final piece of intelligence regarding the budget and schedule overruns on this fictitious project. They were indeed the result of a scope change; however, the scope change was driven by a politician who had done so for political purposes and had demanded the project director follow their instructions. On this basis, despite some misgivings, one or two considered the politician accountable, while others spread the accountability across other role holders in the project.

In my debrief to the executive team I pointed out that the organization had a very large capital budget and that this exercise seemed to indicate that the executive team weren't really sure who was accountable for it. On the one hand their responses to the various scenarios seemed to indicate that they considered accountability varied according to the information to hand – a novel concept. However, even when they had the same information, they didn't hold a common view as to who was accountable, since for each scenario a variety of positions were nominated as accountable. They agreed that this did not seem reasonable or sustainable.

If an organization is to have proper control over its capital budget it is necessary that there be clear accountability for each project within that budget. Using this exercise as the starting point, I was able to develop an appreciation of the importance of accountability within the organization and as the foundation for a new project governance framework.

If the answer is 'yes', then from a project accountability perspective you're in good shape. If the answer is 'no', then you're in good company because many organizations experience difficulty and confusion in this area. One reason for confusion regarding project accountability is that an organization's structure reflects its operational activity, not the capital activity. Were someone to be asked who was accountable for any particular operational activity, it's likely the organizational structure would provide some strong clues since that is the basis of its formulation. The capital side of the business doesn't have that advantage, so assigning accountability for a project requires a little more thought.

Defining accountability

Accountability means being answerable to your superiors. A person held accountable for achieving an outcome on a project, for instance, is answerable in the event the desired outcome is not achieved. Everyone in a project or an organization is accountable for something, irrespective of their level in the organization.

There is a tendency in some quarters towards a view that the CEO (or divisional manager or minister – anyone perceived to be 'at the top') is 'ultimately accountable'. Well yes, that is true up to a point. However, the higher in the organizational structure you go, the broader the accountability becomes. So, for instance, a CEO's accountability may be for the ongoing effective operation of the company. If one small group within the company is not operating effectively, this does not imply the CEO should be held directly accountable. The accountability is more likely to lie with the officer running that group. Similarly, if a project within an overall programme fails, accountability does not necessarily rest with the programme manager. Only when there is systemic failure of projects within a programme could the programme manager be considered accountable.

Programmes versus projects

Programmes are groups of interrelated projects that, in combination, produce benefits for an organization. Current theory proposes that programmes produce outcomes, which lead to benefits, whereas projects produce outputs (OGC, 2007). However, not all projects are necessarily part of a programme, which suggests that projects too must be able to produce outcomes and benefits. When projects are part of a programme, the programme management function has an overarching coordination and management role. Different organizations have very different approaches to the programme management role. Programmes and programme management are referred to throughout the text and the detailed relationship between programme and project governance is addressed in Chapter 7.

In order to address their accountability, individuals undertake certain tasks. The requirement to undertake these tasks defines their responsibilities. Without becoming too prescriptive or theoretical, a person's accountabilities should encompass all their responsibilities since there is little point in making someone responsible for an activity if there is no associated accountability. Thus, an individual may have many responsibilities in the organization that relate to only a few accountabilities.

Accountability must be twinned with the necessary level of authority. Authority empowers a person to achieve an outcome for which they are accountable. Accountability for the outcome must reside with an individual who has vested in them the necessary authority required to achieve that outcome. Accountability cannot be shared without being blurred. This means that a committee cannot be held jointly accountable. Each member of the committee will have individual accountability but the committee as a whole is not accountable.

Accountability in the project governance sense is important because it provides clarity of decision making. Clear accountability ensures that any individual in the project governance arrangements, and for that matter the organization, understands which decisions fall within their remit and which decisions will be made by their colleagues. This doesn't mean that an executive sitting on the project decision-making forum only has input to decisions that fall within their accountability remit, but rather that they know where the accountability for the various decisions lies. Any number of persons can have input to any particular decision, but only one person is accountable for the outcome that the decision delivers.

The principles of effective project governance

Principle 1: Ensure a single point of accountability for the success of the project

It's not unusual for projects to have no clear statements of accountability for the various project roles, such as the project manager and team leaders. Even statements of key responsibilities for these role holders tend to be the exception rather than the rule. Whilst this may not be ideal, the lack of accountability and responsibility statements may not significantly impact either the project or officers' ability to perform on it. This is because the project team, that is, the project manager and those who report to the project manager, usually work together on a daily basis. With teamwork and cooperation it normally becomes apparent when there are either overlaps or gaps, providing of course the project team has been organized into an effective and workable delivery structure. So while the ideal is always to have comprehensive role statements, experienced project people and their projects are unlikely to suffer for the lack of them.

Contrast this with the situation of those involved in the decision-making forum. Their opportunity for teamwork and cooperation is severely curtailed by the infrequency of governance meetings. They may be meeting only once per month, and that may only be for one to two hours. In this situation, a lack of clarity regarding relative accountabilities and responsibilities is not so easily overcome. Coupled with that is the significant resources they are directing on the project that require clarity of decisions and direction, clear objectives, etc., and if the executives on the decision-making forum are unclear of their responsibilities it is likely to be translated into wasted effort on the project. At the project governance level, it is imperative that all concerned have role clarity.

In particular, one accountability within the project governance framework is more important than any other – accountability for the success of the project. The importance of this concept to the project, and indeed the organization, cannot be overstated. A project without a clear understanding of who assumes accountability for its success has no clear leadership. With no clear accountability for project success, there is no one driving the solutions to the difficult issues that beset all projects at some point in their life. Instead the project proceeds along the previously discussed consensus-building approach to decision making with all its attendant inefficiencies. It also slows the project during the crucial project initiation phase, since there is no one person to take the important decisions necessary to place the project on a firm footing. This concept is the first principle of effective project governance.

Principle 1: Ensure a single point of accountability for the success of the project

---

Although this is a necessary requirement, it is insufficient on its own. It is not enough to nominate someone to be accountable – the right person must be made accountable. There are two aspects to this. As discussed above, the person who is accountable must hold sufficient authority within the organization to ensure they are empowered to make the decisions necessary for the project's success. Beyond this, however, is the fact that the right person from the correct area within the organization must be held accountable. If the wrong person is selected, the project is no better placed than if no one was accountable for its success. To determine the single person who will assume accountability for the success of the project requires a more detailed understanding of the relationship between service delivery and asset delivery.

Principle 2: Service delivery ownership determines project ownership

In order to be effective or in some cases even survive, organizations must constantly focus on the service that they are providing. Most organizations deliver services. They either deliver the service first hand, or do so indirectly through the products they produce. Thus, a maker of automotive components provides a service to a car-maker through the products they provide and the manner in which they provide them – quality, timeliness and so on. Similarly, a government roads department builds roads, bridges, interchanges and tunnels. However, these assets are not in themselves fundamentally useful. They are useful only as a means to an end, and that end is the service they provide – access, reduction in travel times, increased driver comfort levels, reduced accident rates, and so on. It is therefore the service that the bridge delivers or enables that defines its worth. If the bridge isn't built in the optimum position or is incorrectly sized, then the service level is compromised, irrespective of the quality of the asset itself. The same can be seen in ICT systems, which are platforms for the delivery of services. It is when ICT organizations or business units forget that they are providing a service and not a system that the relationship between them and the business and business managers fails. The point is it's not so much the product but rather the service the product provides or enables that is the important and fundamental output.

The specification of the services being delivered cannot remain static because the environment within which the organization operates is itself dynamic. There are many factors at play that are acting to diminish the level of service or cause it to deteriorate or become less effective, efficient or competitive. These factors are a function of the broader environment in which the organization operates and will include economic trends, demographics, social trends, legislative changes, etc. There are plenty of examples of environmental factors that can have an impact on an organization's service offerings:

- technological advances may render the service, or the asset that provides the service, obsolete – a constant concern in the high technology consumer sectors;
- the regulatory environment may change and necessitate an increase in service level. An example of this is covered in the electricity sector case study at the end of Chapter 4, where the introduction of competition at the domestic level changed the face of the electricity sector in England and Wales;
- new environmental factors or laws may have an impact on the delivery of the service, such as the law that required the phasing out of chlorofluorocarbons (CFCs) from refrigeration products;
- population increase can have an impact on the level of service provided, with levels deteriorating as assets reach or exceed their capacity. Growing cities face this problem in respect of traffic flows.

So organizations must constantly be planning ahead to maintain service at acceptable levels. When the environment changes, the organization must change with it. If the change within the environment is small, the service may only need tweaking to once again meet the particular needs of the organization's customers. When the environmental change is significant, however, a step response is required from the organization. This may involve the delivery and integration of any combination of new assets, new business processes, new systems and/or new personnel. Significant change in an organization is best achieved with a project or a programme of related projects with an end date determined by the timing of the need for the new service.

The project is the organization's response to the change in the service need, and the project is defined by the service need it enables. The project's primary objective is therefore to deliver a service. In order to achieve this, the project may need to also deliver an asset, but this is only as a means to an end. Fundamentally, projects deliver services, not

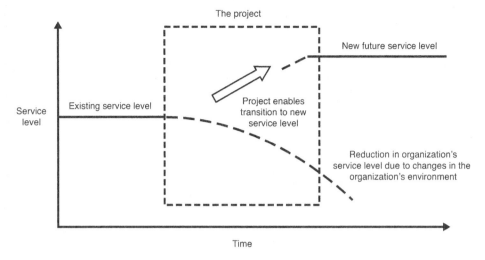

Figure 2.1 The project as a transition mechanism

assets. Assets are enablers of service delivery; they are the platform from which services are delivered.

This concept is displayed in Figure 2.1. The starting point is an organization delivering a level of service. The end point is the organization delivering a new, higher level of service. The transition between the two is effected by a project. The project is the means by which the organization introduced the new service level. This concept is important because it places the project in the context of the service that will be enabled through the asset the project will deliver. The fact that projects primarily deliver services has implications in terms of their ownership and the decision-making framework. Both of these factors determine the project's direction and definition, and drive its delivery. Ownership of the business service confers the right of ownership of the project that will deliver the service. With project ownership comes project accountability. This has major implications when choosing the individual to be held accountable for the success of the project. The owner of services within an organization is of course from the operational side of the business. Accountability for the success of the project must therefore reside with those business owners who have service delivery responsibility. This logic dictates that both the ownership of the project and its decision-making framework should reflect a service delivery focus rather than an asset delivery focus, and that ownership should reside within the operational business unit.

> Projects deliver services rather than just assets. Assets are enablers
> of service delivery

The corollary to this is that the ownership of the project does not reside with those delivering the asset. While the asset may be central to the provision of the services, it does not in itself constitute the service. This concept has implications in important aspects of the project. For instance, a service delivery focus necessitates a whole-of-life project cost perspective since the service itself will have an associated ongoing, post-project, operational cost. A service delivery focus also recognizes that at commissioning the asset must integrate into the existing service regime. On the other hand, if a project is viewed as delivering an asset, the focus is on the capital cost of the asset and operational costs become a secondary consideration, as does serviceability of the outcome.

When the delivery arm of the organization has greater stewardship and ownership of the project than those who will have responsibility for the ongoing operation of the service that the asset enables, project outcomes and service requirements can be mismatched. For example:

- if you consider a project's objective is to deliver a new hospital rather than the provision of health services, then the outcome is potentially a building that doesn't meet the needs of health care professionals, exhibiting high operational costs, and therefore potentially higher whole-of-life costs, due to poor workflow considerations;
- if you consider a project's objective is to deliver an IT system for document and records management, then the outcome may well be a cutting-edge electronic document and records management system (eDRMS) but one with which business users won't engage;
- if you believe a project's objective is to deliver a new roundabout to reduce congestion at an intersection rather than a reduction in urban travel times, the outcome may be a congestion problem transferred a few miles further down the road, with no savings in travel time.

The intention therefore is to determine the ownership of the project by identifying the owner of the service the project will deliver. This approach places the business at the heart of project delivery. While the business may be unable to deliver the project without assistance, it nevertheless is in the role of primary project decision maker, albeit supported as necessary by project delivery specialists. This ensures the project governance framework maintains a service delivery focus. This then is the second principle of effective project governance.

Principle 2: Service delivery ownership determines project ownership

---

It is important to remember that this discussion is purely about project ownership. It does not imply a lesser role on the part of the asset delivery arm of the organization – just a different role. The service delivery arm of the organization must work hand-in-glove with the asset delivery arm for a successful project outcome. How this occurs, and the responsibility breakdown, is discussed in coming chapters.

Principles 1 and 2 are focused on the project's major stakeholder – the owner of the project. Projects have many stakeholders and an effective project governance framework must address their needs. The next principle deals with the manner in which this should occur.

Principle 3: Ensure separation of stakeholder management and project decision-making activities

Most people with experience of committees would agree that the decision-making effectiveness of a committee is inversely proportional to its size. Not only can a large committee fail to make timely decisions, those it does make are often ill-considered because of the particular group dynamics at play.

As project decision-making forums grow in size, they tend to morph into stakeholder management groups. For example, on large, complex projects there can sometimes be in excess of 20 people attending a steering committee meeting. Were each person to be questioned as to why they were there, most would give what appears to be a valid reason for their presence. In some way each of them is a stakeholder on that project, and this of course is the problem. As stated previously, the main role of a project governance body such as a project steering committee (or project board or project control group) is decision making, not stakeholder management. When numbers increase, the detailed understanding of each attendee of the critical project issues reduces. Many of those present attend not to make decisions but as a way of finding out what is happening on the project. The previous chapter discussed the difficulty large committees have in making effective decisions and the problems this can cause. Not only is there insufficient time for each person to make their point, but those with the most valid input must fight for time and influence with those with only a peripheral involvement in the project. Further, not all of those who are present will have the same level of understanding of the issues and so time is wasted bringing everyone up to speed on the particular issues being discussed. Hence, to all intents and purposes, a large project committee is constituted more as a stakeholder management forum than a project decision-making forum. This is a major issue when the project depends on the committee to make decisions.

There is no question here that both activities, project decision making and stakeholder management, are essential to the success of the project. The issue is that stakeholder management and project decision making are two separate activities and need to be treated as such. This is the third principle of effective project governance.

Principle 3: Ensure separation of stakeholder management and project decision-making activities

---

If this separation can be achieved, it will avoid clogging the decision-making forum with numerous stakeholders by constraining its membership to only those select stakeholders absolutely central to its success. There is always the possibility that this solution will lead to a further problem if disgruntled stakeholders do not consider their needs are being met. Whatever stakeholder management mechanism is put in place will have to adequately address the needs of all project stakeholders. It will need to capture their input and views and address their concerns to their satisfaction. These stakeholders must also be confident they have a champion in the decision-making forum who will represent their cause.

Principle 4: Ensure separation of project governance and organizational governance structures

When the causes of ineffective project governance were discussed earlier in this book, the problems associated with multi-layered or hierarchical decision making were raised. These problems were often associated with the melding of project governance and organizational governance. Project governance is established precisely because it is recognized that the organization governance structure does not provide the necessary framework to deliver a project.

Unless, then, it is felt that the project governance framework established for a project is inadequate in some way, there should be no need to integrate it within the organization structure. It is recognized that the organization has valid requirements in terms of reporting and stakeholder involvement. However, dedicated reporting mechanisms established by the project can address the former and the project governance framework must itself address the latter. What should be avoided is the situation where the decisions of the steering committee, project board or project control group are required to be ratified by one or more persons in the organization outside of that project decision-making forum. This becomes the final principle of effective project governance.

Principle 4: Ensure separation of project governance and organizational governance structures

---

Following this principle will minimize multi-layered decision making and the time delays and inefficiencies associated with it. It will ensure a project decision-making body is empowered to make decisions in a timely manner.

This completes the four principles of effective project governance. They will serve as a guide in the development of a project governance model. Also, in the event that circumstances force the modification of the model, the principles will provide the ultimate constraints to the modifications.

Executive summary: The four principles of effective project governance

- Ensure a single point of accountability for the success of the project. This ensures clarity of leadership, plus clarity and time-liness of decision making.
- Service delivery ownership determines project ownership. This places the business at the heart of project delivery and ensures the project governance framework maintains a service delivery focus.
- Ensure separation of stakeholder management and project decision-making activities. This will prevent decision-making forums from becoming clogged with stakeholders, which would result in laboured or ineffective decision making.
- Ensure separation of project governance and organizational governance structures. This will reduce the number of project decision layers, since the project decision path will not follow the organizational line of command. Confusing them results in organizational role accountabilities sitting uneasily alongside project governance accountability needs.

3 Building the project governance model

This chapter develops a project governance model derived from the principles developed in the previous chapter. The four principles of effective project governance make it clear that there is a need to differentiate between stakeholder management and project decision making. This therefore requires a determination of the key project stakeholders needed to form the primary decision-making body. Other stakeholders less central to the project must still have a platform for addressing their issues and concerns but this need not be within the decision-making body.

Key stakeholders and the project board

The project owner

Principle 1 of the four principles of effective project governance requires a single point of accountability for the success of the project. Principle 2 requires that this person have a service delivery focus and be the owner of the project. This person will be referred to as the project owner to clearly indicate their primary responsibility on the project. The project owner's role is summarized in Figure 3.1.

Project owner

• Accountable for the success of the project.
• Holds operational responsibility for service delivery.

Figure 3.1 The project owner

The project owner is the project's most important stakeholder – the individual whose ongoing role in service delivery is dependent upon the successful delivery of the project. This person must therefore be drawn from and represent the business. For example:

- On a major road project the project owner will most likely be a senior executive drawn from the group within the organization with responsibility for the service provided by the major roads network in that area. This person is likely to have overall responsibility in that geographical area for traffic or network operations and maintenance.
- The project owner on information and communications technology (ICT) implementations must represent the business. It is therefore highly unlikely that ownership of such a project should reside within the ICT group itself. For example, project ownership of the implementation of a corporate-wide electronic document and records management system (eDRMS) should probably sit within the corporate area since its impact will be felt over the entire organization. The same logic applies for a human resources (HR) system and the head of HR may be the project owner. If the impact of the ICT implementation is more localized, for instance implementation of a project management tool within a project delivery group, then the project owner will be an executive whose role encompasses project delivery in that group. It may not need to be the head of that group. In most ICT implementations the project owner is normally an executive, or their delegate, who either has organizational responsibility for the impacted business areas or can provide de facto leadership by virtue of their position within a centralized corporate function, such as is the case with the eDRMS implementation.
- A new tertiary hospital will have a major impact on health care in that region. The project owner for such a project may therefore be a

regional health director or possibly the hospital CEO, if that person has been appointed sufficiently early in the project's development.

In the PRINCE2 project management methodology the project owner is referred to as the executive. In the OGC Gateway Process, this role is usually referred to as the senior responsible owner (SRO). There are two further stakeholders that warrant inclusion in the project decision-making forum.

The senior user

The first is a representative of users of the service that the asset will deliver, whether that asset is infrastructure, an IT system or a business process or policy. If users' needs are not adequately met, project success will be compromised, and so users must have adequate representation on the project. This role is referred to as the senior user, utilizing the same terminology as PRINCE2 – refer to the text box 'Terminology' (page 42). Users may be users of the service or users of the asset that enables the service. The senior user may also represent those with an operational interest in the project or those with a maintenance interest. It may be that there is a degree of overlap with the representation provided by the project owner. Although this should be minimized where possible, some overlap is not usually an issue, providing of course it is clear who is filling which role. Where users of the end product are external to the organization or are community based and therefore unsuitable for the senior user role, the role may be held by a key project stakeholder for whom the project is delivering benefits, meeting their objectives or having an impact on their own business activities. Using the same project examples as for the project owner role:

- On the major road project the senior user could be a representative from the traffic or network operations group. Note that it is unlikely that a representative of a motorists' organization (AA, RAC, etc) would fill the role because they are not part of the organization (for instance, government) and therefore are not obliged to act in the organization's best interests and within the constraints set by the project owner. Of course, the motoring organizations will be important stakeholders for the project and need to be managed as such. Their views could be taken on board through their involvement in a user group.

- Identifying the senior user on major ICT implementations can be a challenge when the implementation is corporate wide, for instance the eDRMS system or HR systems. In these situations, because the system impacts on users across the organization, the senior user will need to represent many different business units. For the eDRMS implementation, the corporate HR group could provide the senior user, who is then well positioned to represent impacted parties. It may also be useful to have a second senior user on a project such as this, since so many users are impacted. A second senior user would enable a representation from outside the corporate area.

    In the HR implementation, with HR the likely project owner, they ideally shouldn't fill the senior user role as well. On large projects it helps to get a spread of experience and input from across the organization on the project board and one person or business unit filling two roles won't achieve that. What could work is to have one senior user from outside the corporate area and possibly one from the payroll function. The latter, although probably within the HR function, is the most critical area affected by the project and so their involvement in the project board should be welcome:

- Hospital projects are well known for the wide range of users they encompass and choosing a senior user can be problematic. These projects often have many user groups to ensure full coverage of users' needs. The solution to the senior user role can depend on the structure of the health area. For instance, a new tertiary hospital will have a major impact on health care in the region. The project owner for such a project may therefore be a regional health director rather than the CEO of the hospital or local district. The latter can then step into the senior user role, managing the inputs of the various clinicians, facilities management, etc.

The senior user is accountable for ensuring the needs of the project's users are addressed and has the primary responsibility of defining and monitoring the project's delivery of user requirements. The senior user chairs the project user groups. In certain projects there may be a number of user groups and the senior user will manage their activities, although perhaps not chairing them all. The senior user's role is summarized in Figure 3.2.

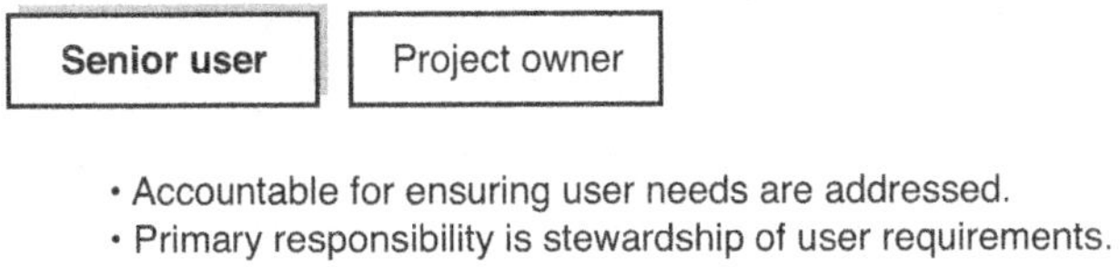

Senior user	Project owner

• Accountable for ensuring user needs are addressed.
• Primary responsibility is stewardship of user requirements.

Figure 3.2 The senior user

The senior supplier

Our stakeholders now include the person who will own the project and a representative of those who will use the service the asset delivers or use the asset itself to deliver services. This provides a team that is very service delivery focused, as was the intent. However, it's necessary to introduce an asset delivery focus to the team – a person whose role it is to ensure the assets or products the project delivers meet the service delivery needs. The key stakeholder in this respect is a representative of the organization that will deliver the assets. This person is referred to as the senior supplier. The senior supplier is accountable for the delivery of the project assets to meet the needs of the senior user and the project owner. The senior supplier's primary responsibility is for design and development of the project's assets, as summarized in Figure 3.3. The holder of this position may change over the course of the project since the services being provided to the project change. The role may also be split in the event that there are both internal and external providers of project delivery services.

For instance, and following the earlier examples, on the major road project the choice of senior supplier will depend on whether there is an in-house provider of project delivery services. If so, a senior executive from that group will provide the senior supplier role. If there is also procurement of external resources, it would be normal for a representative of that entity also to hold a senior supplier position. In the early developmental phase of the project that role may be held by a representative of the consultancy advisor. When the successful tenderer has been announced, it will be more appropriate for a representative of that organization to fill the role. The same concepts hold for both the ICT projects and the hospital project.

Note that under certain contractual arrangements such as a public–private partnership (PPP) or private finance initiative (PFI) the project's supplier may also have responsibility for future operation

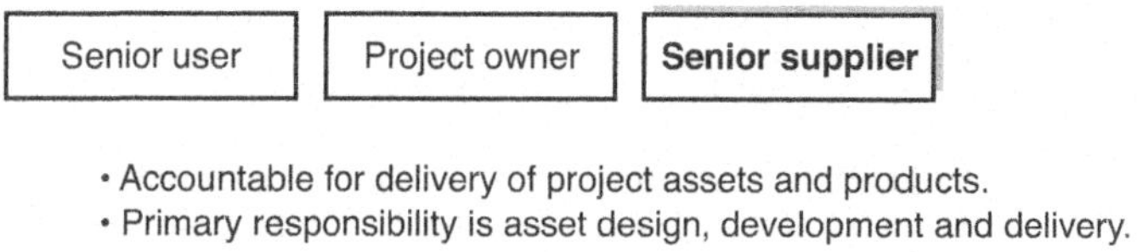

Senior user	Project owner	**Senior supplier**

• Accountable for delivery of project assets and products.
• Primary responsibility is asset design, development and delivery.

Figure 3.3　The senior supplier

and/or maintenance of the asset. Should this be the case, be aware that the senior supplier does not represent the interests of users by virtue of their interest in operations and maintenance. The senior supplier remains a supplier of services and a senior user must be chosen from within the organization to reflect the needs of users of the delivered service. This is not to say the senior supplier will not have an interest in user-related issues, especially around operations and maintenance, and can manage that interest through their senior supplier position on the project board. In general, the project board will need to reflect the particular contractual arrangements pertaining to each PPP.

This cohort forms the project decision-making forum called the project board. The project board contains the key stakeholders representing those groups central to the success of the project:

● the owner of the project, representing the core business of the organization – service delivery;
● a representative of those who will use the asset or service;
● a representative of those who will deliver either services to the project or the asset itself.

Terminology

The terms project board, senior user and senior supplier are taken from PRINCE2 terminology, though it is possible they have also been used in other contexts. The term project owner is used instead of the PRINCE2 term executive or the OGC term senior responsible owner (SRO) since it better reflects the true meaning of the role and its accountability. Generally speaking, these terms have the same meaning as their PRINCE2 equivalents.

The project director

The project director drives the project on behalf of the project owner and provides project delivery experience that may or may not be lacking in the project owner. The greater the project risk, the greater the level of authority required by the project owner. On large, complex, high-risk projects, the project owner position will be held by senior officers within the organization. This raises two issues.

First, due to the demands placed upon these individuals in their day-to-day operational roles, they may not have the necessary time available to devote to the project. This issue is particularly critical given that the project owner is the driving force behind the project. In the project's early stages, the project owner generates the project's momentum and ensures support for it in the organization. The larger and more complex the project, the more likely it is that the time required by the project owner role is incompatible with the time required by the project owner's operational role. In such circumstances it is quite likely the project owner will struggle to offer the project sufficient time.

The second issue is one of skill set. In some environments and organizations, project owners will be highly skilled and experienced in project delivery because it is a regular part of their role; they may work for an organization that regularly delivers significant projects. But this won't always be the case. There will be organizations and circumstances where a project owner is faced with a project whose size and complexity is such that they do not have the requisite skills and experience to deliver it efficiently. Or, they may be adept at delivery of infrastructure projects, for example, but are faced with being project owner of the implementation of an ICT system. It is worth remembering that such executives hold their position within the organization due to their business skills rather than their project delivery skills. In order to overcome the dual problems of project owner time and skill constraints, the new role of project director is introduced to the project board.

The project director reports directly to the project owner and sits on the project board. The project director works closely with the project manager and acts as the primary interface between the business and those delivering the asset. The addition of the project director to the project board completes this committee. There may be support structures in place for individual project board members such as project assurance roles, but these are not part of the decision-making forum. The role of the project director is summarized in Figure 3.4.

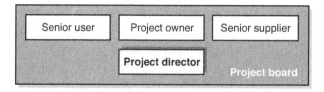

• Accountable to the project owner for ensuring the project owner's needs are met.
• Primary responsibility is to drive the delivery of services for the project owner.
• Provides project delivery expertise to the project owner's team.

Figure 3.4   The project director and the project board

The project board

The project board is established early in the project's life and contains the key stakeholders required to drive project delivery. Members are appointed by the project owner, perhaps with the assistance of corporate or programme management. Where a project is part of an overarching programme of work, it is not unusual for the programme management office to play a part in the selection of project owners. The project owner chairs the board and is the final arbiter for all board decisions. This ensures the project owner has the necessary authority to support their accountability for the success of the project. Clearly the organization needs to ratify the authority of their project owners, which can be achieved through a project governance policy. The senior user and senior supplier support the project owner but in the event of disagreement on a course of action, the project owner's decision prevails. Generally speaking, such a situation is unlikely to occur in practice and any project where disagreement at the project board level is a regular feature is a project with significant issues.

Project board members cannot delegate their accountability and should be wary of delegating their responsibilities. When the latter occurs, there is a risk that the delegates will not have the necessary authority, actual or perceived, to make binding project decisions.

The project board receives reports from the project director and project manager, perhaps jointly. While the project manager reports into the project board, they are not a member of it. The focus of meetings should be on making decisions rather than reporting, and meetings should be arranged around decision-making needs. Having said that, it is recommended that the project board meets sufficiently regularly to ensure the ongoing engagement of project board members.

The project board is responsible for the key project decisions and approves the key project documentation. It also resolves issues escalated by the project manager.

Project board members have stakeholder and relationship management responsibilities. Stakeholder management and the mechanisms that support it will be discussed shortly. However, it is worth commenting first on the different focus that each project board member has. The project owner has overall stakeholder management responsibility and is supported by the other board members generally and the project director specifically. The senior user has primary responsibility for user stakeholder relationships and ensuring consolidated user perspectives are provided to the project board. The senior supplier has primary responsibility for supplier stakeholder relationships.

The project board decisions will revolve around the following main areas, although this is by no means an exclusive list:

- establishment and structuring of the project: the project board should be established shortly after the appointment of the project owner, which itself occurs at project initiation;
- approval of key project documentation: this documentation defines the project and includes the project brief, project plans, business case including preliminary versions, etc;
- resolution of project issues that cannot be resolved by the project director or project manager: there may be issues that the project board itself needs to escalate and this is discussed below;
- important design decisions: the project owner is primarily concerned with the output specification, while the design is the remit of the senior supplier and the project manager. Certain design decisions may have broader impacts on the project, particularly if they have an impact on the broader project community;
- budget: any decisions that have an impact on the budget are within the remit of the project board;
- quality issues: the project's quality standards are a project board responsibility. The initial parameters defining project quality may have been set by an overarching programme or may be derived in part from programme critical success factors (CSFs);
- scope issues: since scope modification normally has an impact on the budget and defines the project, the scope cannot be changed without the approval of the project board;

- time frames and schedules: any changes to the overall schedule or to key milestones within the schedule should be subject to project board approval;
- exceeding or likelihood of exceeding project tolerances: in respect of budget, schedule or quality, the tolerances stipulate the allowable deviation before the project board must report to programme management and, in the case of budget implications, those making investment decisions (which will be discussed shortly). Movements in the project's schedule may have broader implications for the programme, while increases in the budget could raise affordability issues. Decreases in the project budget should also be approved by the project board and, ideally, should be reported to programme management, although there is a natural tendency for projects to treat budget savings as an 'earned' contingency;
- material changes to project plans, etc;
- other specific responsibilities, depending on the project management methodology that is being used.

The terms of reference for the project board are provided in Appendix II.

Investment decision group

The project board is generally not empowered to make the investment decision. In the event the project board approves the business case, it does not necessarily follow that funds will be released to enable the implementation. Project investment decisions affect the ongoing viability of the corporation or organization and as such cannot be made by a project in isolation from corporate management. The project board recommends the investment in the project and supports that recommendation with the business case. The investment decision is made by a group that normally already exists within the organization. For the larger high-risk projects, this group is usually some form of budget committee, known variously by names such as the budget review committee, expenditure review committee, and so on. In this project governance model, this group is referred to as the investment decision group since, for project governance purposes, that is its primary function.

On lower capital value projects, the investment decision group may delegate authority to the programme board or project board. This arrangement may be established when the overarching programme has already received funding approval and the programme board takes on responsibility for approving the investments associated with individual projects within the programme. Alternatively, the investment decision group may delegate investment decisions to a certain value to individual project boards.

In any case, in making its decisions regarding the funding of projects, the investment decision group should act in concert with and be informed by programme management. A project is likely to be a part of a larger programme, and the benefits expected from the overall programme, whilst not accruing to a single project, may be dependent upon its successful completion. Thus uninformed decisions regarding the funding of a single project may have implications for the greater programme.

The structural relationship between the investment decision group, the project board and the project manager and project team is shown in Figure 3.5. The line linking the elements is a decision-making path and decisions are made at each level in the structure.

In a large project there may (or should) be more than one investment decision opportunity. Investment decisions can be structured around progressive iterations of the project business case. The business case

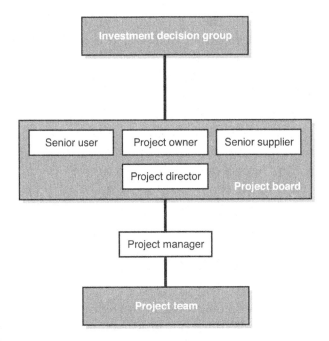

Figure 3.5   The project decision-making path

explains the necessity for the project and shows the balance of its costs and risks against the benefits and services it will deliver. The business case is constructed throughout the project as more work is undertaken and the accuracy of its estimates, time frames and designs is improved. The development of a business case in a large project may itself be a costly exercise – not just in terms of the development costs but also in the corporate and programme management time and focus required. Because of this it is prudent for the organization to make an investment commitment to the development of the full business case, and this falls to the investment decision group.

The business case defines the project and is therefore owned by the project owner, who is responsible for approving it. The investment decision group approves the investment the business case describes.

The membership of the investment decision group is drawn from corporate management. It would normally include one or more of the treasurer, chief financial officer, chief operating officer, select members of the executive management team and ideally should have a representative from programme management. Since the investment decision group may already exist under another guise, it may be that certain meetings are convened as 'investment decision group' meetings and additional members called in as necessary. The project owner should normally present the business case to the investment decision group when an investment decision for that project is on the agenda.

In addition to budget approvals, the investment decision group may also be called upon to resolve issues that cannot be resolved at the project board level. This reflects the seniority and authority of those sitting on this group. These issues are most likely to reflect stakeholder difficulties or impacts on the broader community. The investment decision group may also be called upon to make determinations in relation to matters of corporate policy impacted by the project, an area that again is beyond the remit of the project board. Terms of reference for the investment decision group are provided in Appendix II.

Addressing the needs of other stakeholders

The model as shown in Figure 3.5 is lean and efficient and contains the most important project stakeholders, but in its current form it excludes many other potential stakeholders. If the principle of separate decision-making and stakeholder management functions is to work effectively, the needs of the stakeholders must be adequately addressed or else stakeholders who could be valuable assets to the project may become liabilities. It's therefore necessary to incorporate a stakeholder management function into the model. Note that the stakeholders referred to are those who have a professional or work-related interest in the project rather than individual members of the community or their representatives who are affected by the project. The engagement of community stakeholders is a separate matter and not addressed here.

Stakeholders have the following broad needs:

- to have their opinions sought and to have their views heard;
- to be able to raise issues and concerns and see those issues being addressed and resolved by the project;
- to be able to help shape the project.

Political stakeholders have additional needs, driven by their special relationship with the community:

- they need to be kept abreast of any planned project developments that could affect the community;
- they must be informed as soon as possible of unplanned project developments that have a negative impact on the community;
- they require a timetable of project 'announceables' – those milestones that can be announced to the community to show progress made on the project.

If these stakeholder needs are to be adequately met, it is clear that stakeholders must have a very close relationship with the project and the project board. Stakeholders can be loosely categorized into two groups – senior stakeholders whose support is crucial to the success of the project, and more technical stakeholders with a greater interest in the detailed workings of the project. The first group is referred to as the strategic advisors' group.

Strategic advisors' group

The strategic advisors' group contains the dominant project stakeholders who do not sit on the project board – those individuals who operate at a strategic level and can have a significant impact on the success of the project, whether positive or negative, will be members of this group. Note that these are stakeholders both internal to the organization and associated with external organizations. They are not community stakeholders or members of the public.

The strategic advisors group will normally have representatives from the following stakeholder categories:

- senior managers from organizations contributing to project funding who do not sit on the project board;
- treasury and/or finance;
- other central agency representatives (in the case of government), or representatives from corporate or head office (in the private sector);
- jurisdictions that will be affected by the project;
- senior managers from agencies or organizations that will be affected by the project;
- representatives from other projects that are affected by the project;
- a representative from programme management.

The strategic advisors' group is the forum in which those stakeholders not represented on the project board can raise issues and concerns directly with the project owner. It is not the only reporting mechanism established for these stakeholders – the project owner, project director and project manager should establish reporting and communication protocols to keep these stakeholders up to date on project developments. Additionally, it is expected that the project owner and project director will have regular meetings with individual members of the group.

In order to provide a strong conduit from the strategic advisors' group into the project board, the project owner will chair this group. In this manner, any issue raised by strategic stakeholders will immediately have the attention of the project's main decision maker. Furthermore, there may be a natural tendency for some stakeholders within the strategic advisors' group to desire a seat on the project board. With the project owner chairing both groups, this situation should be eased. The project owner may want the project director and/or the project manager to be involved in strategic advisors' group meetings.

The strategic advisors' group reviews and provides input to project documentation and advises on project issues. Meetings are an opportunity for these stakeholders to shape the project and raise any concerns they may have. Normally, strategic advisors group meetings will be held ahead of project board meetings and meet with the same frequency.

The strategic advisors' group is not strictly a project decision-making forum, but clearly the project will operate more effectively if this group can provide a consolidated position on the main issues facing the project and on any documentation that the project produces and provides for review and input. In the event that agreement cannot be reached between group members, the project owner will take the issue to the project board for resolution and if necessary flag it as an issue for the investment decision group. While there is not the same driver for containing numbers within this group, a manageable size is unlikely to exceed a dozen or so stakeholders. Those with a more peripheral involvement not warranting a seat at the table can be represented by existing members of the strategic advisors' group in order to contain numbers. Also, not all stakeholders will have an interest in all issues raised at the strategic advisors' group. Terms of reference are provided in Appendix II.

A note on alternates

Irrespective of best intentions, project board members, or members of other project governance committees will not be able to attend every meeting. While this situation is unavoidable, it is clearly beneficial for those that fill key roles to maintain continuity on the project. The more that role continuity is compromised, the less effective meetings become.

The worst-case scenario is losing a key role holder well into the project, and their replacement questioning the various positions that have been reached on the project. Two mechanisms can minimize this. First, the project needs to maintain a good record of decisions made. Project board minutes should always clearly and unambiguously state decisions reached. A project board that is not making and recording decisions is not operating effectively. In particular, key project documents need to be signed off when they are approved.

Second, it is incumbent upon role holders to brief fully their respective organizations. In particular, they should always identify an alternate, or substitute, who will take their place in the event that they are unavailable, thereby maintaining continuity. This of course requires that the role holder keep the alternate appraised of project developments.

Stakeholder working group

Those stakeholders operating at a more detailed level within the project environment or with less direct influence may have their needs addressed within a stakeholder working group. This forum addresses the needs of those with more of a technical involvement in the project, as opposed to a strategic involvement. These people may work for members of the strategic advisors' group, who may direct their activities and require them to ensure that stakeholder strategies are adequately implemented on the project. This group is chaired by the project director, thereby providing it with a direct link to the project.

Members of the stakeholder working group will often report to members of the strategic advisors' group within their host organizations. Hence there should be a free flow of information between the two groups. Members of this group will be responsible for ensuring any specific project requirements stipulated by their superiors in the strategic advisors' group are implemented. The terms of reference of the stakeholder working group are provided in Appendix II.

The complete project governance model is shown in Figure 3.6. The key features of the model can be summarized as follows:

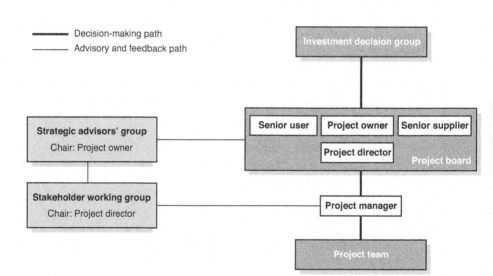

Figure 3.6 The project governance model

- Accountability for the success of the project sits with the project owner, who chairs the project board and the strategic advisors group.
- The decision-making path – the thicker black line in the diagram – is well defined and separate from stakeholder management activities and the tasks of consultation, briefing, reporting, etc.
- The project governance structure is separate to that of the organizational structure. Organizational decision making plays no part in project decision making under this model. Note though that the holders of key organizational roles may sit within the strategic advisors group and provide valuable input to and remain briefed on project developments. The structure recognizes, however, that the decision-making path is via the project board.

Decision making in the project governance model

The majority of the decisions made on a project are made at the project team/project manager level. These people are working with the project day in and day out and making decisions as to the best way forward. Key decisions are made at the project board level around key documentation and issues. Investment, policy and perhaps strategic decisions are made at the investment decision group. Quantifying this, in very broad terms, results in a picture that resembles the following:

- investment decision group: perhaps 1 per cent of project decisions;
- project board: perhaps 4 per cent of project decisions;
- project manager and project team: perhaps 95 per cent of project decisions.

- The intention should be to limit the size of the project board to six persons. Its size is limited by defining the roles that sit within it although some roles may have more than one person filling them.

Mapping the principles to the solution criteria

The criteria that an effective project governance framework must meet were summarized in chapter 1. The following mapping indicates the extent to which the principles of effective project governance along with the project governance model meet these criteria.

The project governance framework must be clear in its objectives. It must fundamentally address project decision making but must also address the structure that enables stakeholder management to be addressed.

The governance model and the principles specifically address project decision making and stakeholder management and are clear on how each function is achieved.

It must enable efficient and effective project decision making. In doing so, it must address issues such as multi-layered decision making resulting from organizational chain of command considerations as well as the tendency towards consensus decision making.

The model and principles separate project decision-making fora from the organization structure, thereby minimizing the issues associated with multi-layered decision making. In separating project decision making and stakeholder management they ensure a lean project board, thereby minimizing the problem of consensus decision making. The project board nonetheless contains the primary project stakeholders, while secondary stakeholders have a mechanism for addressing their needs. These factors should result in improved efficiency and effectiveness.

It must provide clarity of accountability and clear and correct assignment of accountability.

There is no doubt that this has now been achieved. With the project owner as chair of the project board there is clear accountability for the success of the project. Other project board members are aware of their accountabilities. There is also confidence regarding the means of identifying the individuals best placed to be project board members.

It must resolve the relationship between the organization's structure and the temporary structure put in place to deliver the project.

This is the same issue as that addressed above and has been dealt with through the separation of project and organizational governance.

It must support the project delivering a service rather than just an asset, since an asset is only a platform for delivering a service.

Principle 2 addresses this.

It must ensure that those stakeholders who comprise the project's decision-making forum are those necessary to meet the needs of the project without having so many stakeholders in the decision-making forum as to reduce its effectiveness.

This has been achieved through careful identification of the role filled by each project board member and limiting membership to around six persons.

It must ensure that those stakeholders not included within the decision-making forum have their needs adequately met by the project governance framework.

The principles recognize this as necessary and the project governance model provides the mechanism.

The project governance framework must support the efficient and effective initiation of projects.

Effective project initiation requires that the person accountable for the success of the project be identified early in the project's life. It also requires that this person be given the necessary authority to make decisions. The project owner meets this criteria and it is the responsibility of the organization to ensure they are given the necessary authority. The project owner must be identified early in the project.

The project governance framework should support the effective operation of the purchaser/provider model.

The project governance principles and model clarify the different roles of the purchaser and provider. They make clear how the two roles work together. They therefore should improve the operation of the purchaser/provider model within an organization.

The solution criteria have therefore been met by the combination of the four principles of effective project governance and the project governance model.

Executive summary: The project governance model

The project governance model is shown in Figure 3.6. Its key features are:

- project owner: accountable for the success of the project;
- senior user: accountable for ensuring user needs are addressed;
- senior supplier: accountable for delivery of project assets and products;
- project director: accountable to the project owner for ensuring their needs are met;
- the above constitute the project board, which is the primary decision-making body;
- there may be more than one senior supplier and/or senior user;
- the project board should be a maximum of six persons;
- the investment decision group makes funding decisions and resolves escalated issues;
- the strategic advisors' group represents remaining senior stakeholders;
- the strategic advisors group is chaired by the project owner;
- the stakeholder working group represents less senior stakeholders, normally direct reports of strategic advisors' group members.

4 Populating the project board

The project governance framework is only effective with the right person in each role. Appointing the wrong person to any particular role can cause significant damage to the project. This chapter provides guidelines for identifying the person best placed to fill each role within the key decision-making forum, the project board.

Project owner

Identifying the project owner

At the centre of the project governance structure and chair of the project board is the project owner. The project owner is accountable for the success of the project and the title reflects that important accountability. The project owner represents the business and is the individual within the organization whose business unit will utilize the outcomes the project delivers. Hence, the project owner must have a service delivery focus. In the vernacular of the purchaser/provider model, the project owner must be a representative of the purchaser – they are a purchaser of project delivery services and have a customer perspective. To enable this purchasing function the project budget necessarily resides within the customer or business operations area within the organization.

Accountability for the success of a project is closely linked to budget responsibility. If an officer has budget responsibility they are held accountable for that budget. If the budget is expended on a project then it follows that the accountability extends to the outcome delivered by the project. After all, a project is simply a means of adding value to the budget. Since the budget will normally, and should, reside within the business operations area of the organization, it follows that the manager responsible for the business operations that the project will deliver should have accountability for the success of the project. This then places the business at the heart of any project governance framework with the relevant business manager assuming the position of project owner. Note, however, that project accountability does not have to reside precisely with the officer who has delegated financial responsibility but rather within that area of the organization. The former becomes too restrictive when choosing candidates for the project owner role.

The project owner must have project budget responsibility. The project owner is from the purchaser or customer side of the organization and this will normally be where the budget for the project resides. If the project budget does not reside with the area most closely identified with the project owner role, this may reflect a serious flaw in the structuring of the organization. If the project owner is to be held accountable for the success of the project they must have the requisite authority. This requires control over the key decisions affecting the project and these decisions normally revolve around questions of scope, budget, time frames and quality. If the budget lies outside their control their authority and empowerment is compromized. It is not possible to be an effective project owner and not own the project budget. Organizations can get this wrong. It may occur during major reorganizations or restructuring when budget control is split from service delivery. Alternatively this situation can arise through the budget being handed to the asset/project delivery business unit to deliver what they believe the business unit requires. This situation can arise as a response by the organization to project budget overruns by the service delivery group.

In the event of multiple sources of funding for a project, the project owner would normally be the largest contributor. If funding is evenly split between a number of parties, it may be sensible to choose the project owner from that agency or area whose aspects of the project are the most complex or have the greatest element of risk, since this will be the group that has the most difficult decisions to make on the project. It is important to avoid having multiple project owners. This blurs accountability and confuses the decision-making process. It may be possible, when there are two groups with equal claim on the project owner role, for one group to fill a senior user position and thereby maintain close involvement in the project as well as a position on the project board in that manner.

The organization should never outsource the project owner role. It should always remain a core staff position. The project owner role is representing the core business of the organization and is accountable for a project that must integrate with that business. To outsource such a role runs a high risk that the delivered project may not reflect the business needs.

Clearly the person chosen to fill this role must have a level of authority commensurate with the importance of the project to the organization. Large, complex projects require project owners drawn from senior management. A project considered mission-critical may have the CEO as the project owner.

It will obviously be beneficial if the project owner is proficient in the delivery of projects; however; this may not always be the case. Some organizations only occasionally undertake major projects and their executives aren't chosen on the basis of their project delivery ability. It is preferable to choose the project owner on the criteria discussed above and augment their project delivery skills in other ways, such as with the appointment of a skilled project director.

Responsibilities of the project owner

The project owner is responsible for ensuring the project meets the service delivery requirements. This encompasses ensuring the project meets its stated objectives and delivers the promised benefits. In the early stages of the project, the project owner must ensure the project has an articulated set of drivers, an agreed set of objectives and that the benefits the project is seeking to deliver are defined and achievable. Both benefits and objectives must be agreed with the project stakeholders, although not every stakeholder will have an interest in every objective or benefit. Throughout the project's life, the project owner is responsible for ensuring the project remains on track to meet the objectives and deliver these benefits, or else take corrective action.

A project is defined by its business case and therefore the project owner owns the business case and is responsible for ensuring it reflects the service delivery and business needs of the organization. They are responsible for its development and must approve it and any changes that are made to it once it is approved. The business case will be used as the main tool for securing funding for the project from the investment decision group. As such, the project owner should present the business case to the investment decision group at the funding decision point. In the event that the organization's project development process requires that a preliminary business case or similar document be approved by the investment decision group to secure funding for development of the full business case, the project owner will own that document and be responsible for its development and subsequent presentation to the investment decision group.

The project owner is responsible for establishing the project structure. The project board should be established early in the project. The investment decision group will no doubt already exist within the organization, albeit perhaps under another name. The project owner will decide when it is appropriate to constitute the stakeholder committee(s). Other groups or committees may evolve over time, including special working groups, user groups and so on.

Since the project governance structure separates stakeholder management and project decision making it is important to have a mechanism to ensure that this separation does not lead to disconnection between the two. If stakeholders believe that their needs are not being met by the project or that their concerns are not being addressed, the project may fail or not deliver to its potential. Thus the project owner is the primary conduit between the strategic advisors' group and the project board and chairs both bodies. Further, the project owner must establish project reporting and communications protocols such that project stakeholders both internal and external to the organization are kept appraised of project progress and major risks and issues. The project owner will be the main champion and sponsor of the project both within the organization and externally, and the most obvious manifestation of this is the project owner's chairing of the strategic advisors' group.

The project owner appoints project board members in consultation with programme management and/or senior management. In particular, the project owner sources and selects the project director, who will represent the project owner's interests in the day-to-day running of the project and liaise closely with the project manager. The project owner should agree with each member of the project board their project responsibilities. In particular, the project owner will need to agree with the project director the split of responsibility between the two and the delegated authority of the project director. The greater the responsibility and authority delegated to this position, the less the project workload on the project owner. However, a suitable balance must be obtained to ensure the project owner has sufficient engagement to fulfil their accountability on the project.

The project owner must work closely with the project director so that the latter has the necessary understanding of the project owner's needs in relation to the project. This is particularly important in circumstances where the project director may be sourced from outside the organization. The project owner will need to provide advice and direction to the project director.

Since the project owner is accountable for the success of the project, all decisions made at the project board level must be ratified or agreed by the project owner; if the project owner does not agree, it is not a project board decision. These decisions include:

- approval of key project documents, including the preliminary and final business case;
- agreed positions on key issues;
- approval of any material changes to agreed documentation. One measure of materiality is any change that can, or in the future is likely to, impact the business case;
- recommendations on matters escalated to the investment decision group;
- major design decisions.

The project owner will necessarily be involved in the resolution of conflicts both internal to the project and external. Internal conflicts may arise between members of the project team, who may comprise a mixture of consultancies/contractors and client teams, not all of whom may be comfortable working in an integrated team. Team members will bring different perspectives to the project, representing, as they do, the potentially competing views of users, suppliers and owner. These views must be balanced and melded and the project owner will have a key role, working with fellow project board members, to achieve this. Conflicts between stakeholders and between stakeholders and the project team may arise due to disparate objectives or the means by which common objectives are being achieved. Continual communication and early and clear statement of project objectives will go some way towards avoiding such conflict. In the event that external conflicts cannot be resolved at the project board level, it may be necessary for the project board/project owner to escalate these to senior management or the investment decision group.

Finally, the project owner will close the project. This should entail a formal review of the business case and a reconciliation of the project outcomes with the stated objectives and desired benefits stipulated in that document. This is also an opportunity for the lessons learned on the project to be captured and forwarded to programme management. On large and complex projects with long time frames, the 'lessons learned' process needs to be undertaken at perhaps two stages during the project – at or around the time of the investment decision, and then subsequent to project commissioning.

The project owner will require owner resources in order to fulfil their responsibilities. It is the responsibility of the project owner to ensure that sufficient owner resources are available to the project to meet both their needs and the needs of the project.

Skills and attributes of the project owner

First and foremost, the project owner must have a comprehensive understanding of the business and the business drivers for the project. This need is met in large through the project owner being drawn from the service delivery or customer side of the organization. Additionally, the project owner must be able to view the project in the broader context of the programme or organization, understanding the dependencies between this project and others that comprise the programme or are being addressed by the organization. Where the project is sufficiently large, a strong grasp of its interactions with the broader economic, political (where necessary) and social environment will be necessary.

Clearly, the project owner needs to have an understanding of projects and the manner in which they are developed. At the very least, they should understand the concepts of the project development lifecycle and the various key documents that populate that lifecycle. Hence an understanding of the purpose of the business case is essential. It is difficult to envisage a project owner who does not understand a project plan or risk register, or the importance of these documents to the project. The same logic applies to other key documents the project will develop – feasibility studies, options analysis and so on.

The level of knowledge and understanding required is tempered by the role of the project director, who is expected to be highly skilled in the delivery of large projects. The project owner's knowledge of project delivery must be necessarily higher if, for whatever reason, a project director is not engaged on the project.

Project owners will need the ability to develop strong working relationships with, and between, various stakeholders. This includes the ability to bring together the various groupings that will comprise the project team, recognizing that on a large project there may be legal, commercial and technical advisors along with the client team. It is likely the project owner will require negotiating skills and, ideally, be a motivator and leader. The latter, while ideal, is not essential since the project director and project manager will also be providing project leadership, and the desirability of this personality trait should not drive the identification of the project owner. Similarly, while it undoubtedly helps if the project owner has the right interpersonal skills to lead a project, this is a secondary consideration when compared to the primary criteria.

There will be situations where business units with little experience of project delivery find themselves with a large one-off project to deliver in order for the business to continue to meet its service requirements. In such circumstances, it is still essential that the business itself owns the project. The project owner may source the project director from outside the organization, but the project owner role must be from the business, irrespective of project delivery expertise. If necessary, the project owner can attend training or coaching in the fundamentals of this skill. It also makes sense for the project owner to acknowledge their knowledge and skill shortcomings and ensure these gaps are filled by suitable personnel selections in both the project board and the project team.

What is necessary is that the project owner be fully engaged in the project and accessible to the project director and project manager. Not only does this ensure that business needs continue to drive the project, it is essential if the project owner is to be accountable for the success of the project.

Appendix III contains role descriptions for the project owner and other project board roles.

Project initiation

Chapter I discussed the project initiation process and queried what event triggered this process. The answer should now be clearer and is tied to accountability. Until one person has been made accountable for the success of the project, there is no one person with the incentive and authority to drive delivery. Thus the trigger for project initiation is the appointment of the project owner. Subsequent activities in the initiation process include establishment of the project governance arrangements for the project, sourcing of the project director and project manager, and the development of a high-level brief and plan that describes the project and its implementation. But if there is one event that can be said to trigger the commencement of a project, it is the appointment of the project owner.

Senior user

Identifying the senior user

The senior user represents those who will use the final product or service that the project delivers. The role also represents those whom the project may impact in some way – this could be an impact on operations or maintenance activities. In projects that have more than one funding body, the project owner is normally chosen as a representative of the main funding organization and it may be necessary to find a project board position for a representative of the other funding agency(s). Since it is bad practice to appoint more than one project owner due to the blurring of accountability that this will entail, it may be useful to use the senior user position to address this need. The senior user may therefore represent an organization that is contributing to the funding of the project.

Given the variety of needs the senior user role may be filling, it is quite likely the role could be split between two persons. The larger and more complex the project, the more likely this is to be the case. It is not recommended splitting the role between more than two persons since not only does this begin to increase the size of the project board beyond six, it also starts to fragment the accountabilities and responsibilities of the senior user role. On projects with a variety of users, the senior user may have the task of representing business units that either do not report to them or are not part of the same organization as themselves. For instance, the senior user may be representing bodies responsible for future maintenance or operations of the asset, facilities management, and so on, where each activity may be undertaken by a different organization or by different business units within the same organization. (To accommodate these various interests may require more than one user group.) There is no reason why the senior user can't represent each body, given sufficient support, providing conflict of interest issues can be avoided. Apart from appointing a second senior user, another option is to outsource the senior user role and contract an independent person to represent all users and chair user group meetings. Remember too that the project owner may well be representing the interests of more than one organization in the case of multiple sources of funding. And, as will shortly be discussed, it would not be unusual for the senior supplier also to be representing several suppliers to the project.

In order to adequately represent users, the senior user will need a good understanding of the needs of users and will invariably be drawn either from the user community itself or from a business unit that represents the needs of the user community. Note that reference to the user community is referring to organizations or business units within organizations rather than the broader public community even though the latter may be an end user. The implicit assumption is that within the stakeholder organizations there will be officers whose role involves representing the interests of the community at large.

Responsibilities of the senior user

The senior user will be responsible for establishing the user group, negotiating and developing the user requirements and consolidating them into a user requirement document. The user requirement should be formally signed off by the senior user as a key project document. The focus of the user requirement should be on the outputs and outcomes that users need, rather than any specification of the detail of the project itself. In this respect the senior user has a similar focus to the project owner – service delivery – albeit from a user perspective.

Having established user requirements, it is the responsibility of the senior user to ensure the project progresses towards delivery of those requirements throughout its lifecycle. User requirements come at a price and it will be necessary for the senior user to bring to the attention of the other project board members that the higher initial costs of meeting certain user requirements may well be balanced by lower whole-of-life costs. The project owner will balance supplier interests and user interests, as well as costs and quality. The senior user is responsible for presenting the user case in these discussions.

The senior user will have an active involvement in the development of user acceptance testing, particularly on ICT projects. The role will also ensure that user training and user documentation are adequately addressed.

Meeting these responsibilities may require additional user project resources. The senior user is responsible for identifying the need for these resources, defining their responsibilities and committing them to the project. The senior user will need to have a sufficient level of authority within the organization to commit such resources.

Skills and attributes of the senior user

The senior user will ideally be someone known and respected within the user community or must be prepared and able to become so. They may need to be able to negotiate a common agreement on user requirements, some of which may be conflicting, across a range of stakeholders. On projects with large and/or disparate user communities this will necessitate strong negotiation skills.

Senior supplier

Identifying the senior supplier

The senior supplier represents the suppliers of services to the project and provides their perspective and expertise. The services in question will depend on the project and the particular stage in the project's lifecycle. These services may include advisory, transaction, design, ICT, and construction services. The services may be provided by an in-house service provider or an external provider or both, possibly with the in-house provider managing the external contract. In this situation, the senior supplier role could be shared by the in-house provider and the main external supplier of project services. It is preferable that external providers have a seat at the project board even if their input is being managed by an internal service provider, or else the project owner is in danger of being isolated from the main supplier of services to the project and receiving only second-hand knowledge of supplier-related issues. It is not recommended to have more than two persons sharing the senior supplier role even when there may be a number of service providers working on the project since this can unbalance the project board and give it too great an asset delivery focus. To regain the balance then requires the addition of more owner and user representatives and the project board becomes too large.

When there are a number of external suppliers it will be necessary to identify one, or perhaps two, to sit on the project board. The choice of senior supplier in these circumstances becomes a question of their stake in the project, including the size of the various work packages assigned to each supplier, their ability to commit resources to the project and the risk allocation between suppliers and the client organization. The ability to commit resources is of course key since it is primarily by way of suppliers' resources that the project develops. It is important that the senior supplier is not a figurehead from the supplier organization, but instead is someone committed to and engaged with the project.

In some environments there may be resistance in the client organization to having a representative of the supplier sitting on the project board. Such resistance may focus on the need for confidentiality of client commercial matters. However, any matters requiring confidentiality can always be addressed outside of the project board meeting in the absence of the senior supplier. Under normal circumstances it is important that suppliers are represented on the project board. This arrangement allows the project owner to be immediately aware of any issues suppliers may have in respect of any project board decision and, conversely, ensures the senior supplier is aware of the project owner's perspective on any issue. It ensures the project owner, senior user and senior supplier are, to the extent possible with their different perspectives, locked in step on the project.

Once the main project contract has been let, the services provided to the project change from being of a consultancy nature to being of a build or construction nature. At this point, the person filling the senior supplier's role may change to reflect the different services being provided to the project. This is unlike the other positions on the project board where consistency over the course of the project is preferable, particularly in respect of the project owner, where project accountability is a central feature of the role and transferring accountability is challenging.

It is possible that the senior supplier and the project manager will have a business relationship and it may be that the project manager is a direct report of the senior supplier in the supplier's organization. This is not necessarily the case of course since the project manager may have been independently sourced by the project owner or project director. Remember, the project manager reports to the project board rather than to the senior supplier in matters associated with project decision making. However, where the project manager does report to the senior supplier in the supplier organization, this arrangement may well translate into the day-to-day operation of the project, with the project manager referring issues to the senior supplier. The important thing to remember is that key decisions are made and issues resolved by the project board rather than by the senior supplier in isolation.

Responsibilities of the senior supplier

The senior supplier is responsible for ensuring the necessary supplier resources are committed to the project. This means not only the resources of that particular supplier, but also the resources of all suppliers involved in the project. This is one reason why when the project moves from the development or design phase to the construction phase, it is quite likely that the senior supplier needs to change also. A consultancy advisor will be unable to commit contractor resources.

The senior supplier advises and informs the project board of supplier perspectives on the matters the board addresses. This includes providing supplier impact assessments of changes to specifications or to the project's business case, or of decisions taken or considered by the project board. Similarly, any supplier issues that could have an impact on the achievement of business or user requirements, or on the business case, should be raised by the senior supplier.

The quality of outputs and products provided by suppliers is also the responsibility of the senior supplier. In its simplest form this entails ensuring that supplier deliverables meet specified standards. The senior supplier may or may not have contracts with all suppliers on the project. Where they don't, the project owner will have such contracts in place and so the senior supplier will need to work closely with the project owner in managing these suppliers.

The project owner, senior user and other key stakeholders may not have a complete grasp of the technology the project will utilize or the more technical aspects of the project. Usually, it will be the senior supplier who has access to the requisite level of knowledge and it is their responsibility to interpret technical complexity to ensure that project stakeholders have the necessary level of understanding to make informed decisions.

Skills and attributes of the senior supplier

The senior supplier will need to recognize that the project's objectives revolve around service delivery outcomes rather than asset delivery alone. Thus there may be occasions when project board decisions favour the former rather than the latter and the senior supplier will need to appreciate the reasons why this is the case.

The senior supplier will need to be a technically competent person with project management skills. They will be experienced in the type of project being delivered, probably having undertaken project management roles at some time in the past. The senior supplier will necessarily have a level of authority in the supplier organization and amongst other suppliers to enable them to commit their own organization's resources and influence other suppliers to do the same, especially at times when resources additional to those initially estimated are required. The senior supplier will benefit from being a good communicator, including being able to explain complex technical matters to non-technical stakeholders.

A note to consultants/contractors: Customers who are not project owners

A contractor's client in an organization is, by definition, their customer. However, their customer may not be the project owner as defined in this book. Where in this book the term customer or purchaser has been used, it is referring to the project owner. Where the project owner's organization has an in-house service provider (and most large organizations do), it is likely that contractors in particular will be sourced through that entity. If this is the case then the contractor's customer in this circumstance is the in-house service provider rather than the project owner. Thus the contractor's customer and the project's customer (the project owner) are different entities. In fact, it may be that the contractor's client/customer in such circumstances is the senior supplier.

Project director

The project director undertakes day-to-day management for and makes decisions on behalf of the project owner. This role supports the project owner and reflects the reality that 1) the project owner may not be able to devote themselves full time to the project, and 2) the project owner may not have the necessary skill set to deliver a major project. The project director therefore works closely with the project owner and must have a clear understanding of the project owner's requirements and service delivery needs to ensure the project owner's business case is delivered in the form of the completed project. The project director also works closely with the project manager to ensure service delivery outcomes are met. This cannot be left to the project manager who while delivering the project to the project owner's requirements is nevertheless focused on asset delivery. (Unusually, but not always, in the early planning phase of a project, the project manager may be a project owner resource.)

The project director's role may change during some projects. For instance, on construction projects much of the transactional complexity of the project is involved in the early stages as the project builds its business case and works with its stakeholders to arrive at an agreed and sustainable project. The project is then taken to the market, market responses are assessed and an investment decision is made. The skill set required for these activities is quite different to those required for subsequent activities during the construction phase. The latter role becomes more of an owner's engineer or customer's representative than a project director in the sense referred to here and it may be that a change of personnel is needed at this point to reflect the different skill set required.

Identifying the project director

The project director provides the interface between project ownership and delivery. The project director represents the project owner and therefore the business and acts as the main point of contact with the project manager for the day-to-day management of business interests. The project director is responsible for ongoing management on behalf of the project owner to ensure that the desired project objectives are delivered. This person must have adequate knowledge and information about the business and the project to be able to make informed decisions. They must also be experienced in project delivery, preferably with a project management background.

The project director should be sourced by the project owner. If the delivery or supplier side of the project sources the project director there will inevitably be confusion surrounding the role's accountability and responsibilities. The project owner can source the project director either internally or externally. Given that project management is a core skill of the project director, such expertise may be more readily found in the delivery side of the business rather than the customer or operations side. Delivery side sourcing can work providing it is viewed as a secondment and that all parties acknowledge that the reporting line is to the project owner. The personal contractual arrangements of any secondment will need to reflect this reporting line since delivery side performance measures remaining on the project director's contract would likely make the role untenable. The project director can be externally sourced by the project owner. This approach ensures there is no confusion about who the project director reports to, but the outsourced project director has to be brought up to speed on the business and its needs.

On smaller projects, the roles of project owner and project director may be combined. It is inadvisable to combine the project director and project manager roles since although the relevant skill sets are similar, the former must approach the project from a service delivery perspective, whereas the latter usually does so from an asset delivery perspective.

Government can have difficulty recruiting good project directors since the best ones, needed for the largest and most complex projects, will charge accordingly and often therefore do not easily fit within governments pay scales. It may be possible to capitalize the project director's costs. The cost of a good project director is likely to be small in comparison to the savings and benefits they can bring to the project and organization.

Responsibilities of the project director

It is important the project director and project owner work together to agree the project director's responsibilities, since in many respects the project director's role is a subset of that of the project owner's. Remember that the project director's role exists primarily to address either gaps in the project owner's skill set (ie project delivery) or their availability to properly manage the project along with their other responsibilities. It will be up to the project owner to decide what responsibility they wish to delegate to the project director. The arrangement is described diagrammatically in Figure 4.1.

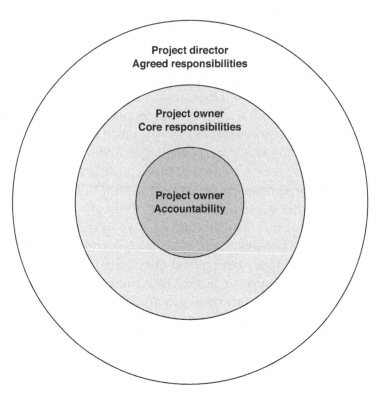

Figure 4.1 Project owner/director responsibility split

The project director should be involved in the establishment of the project team. This necessitates the project director's position being established early in the project and ideally ahead of any consultant or contractor procurement activity. In particular the project director will have a keen interest in the selection of the project manager since this is a person they will be working closely with over the course of the project.

The project director will liaise closely with the project owner and will need to ensure the project owner and other stakeholders are kept fully informed of the progress of the project. Note that the project owner chairs the strategic advisors' group and so will either provide that group with progress reports or will require the project director to attend strategic advisors' group meetings to provide such reports. The project director chairs the stakeholder working group and therefore reports on progress and issues to this group. The project owner will expect reporting to be a central service provided by the project director and so the project director is responsible for establishing reporting arrangements designed to meet the needs of stakeholders external to the project. Project directors are assisted in this task by the project manager who themselves will provide detailed project progress reports.

The project director will act as the project manager's main point of contact with the client organization and the project manager will expect the project director to address client issues, including working with end users to assist them in providing their inputs to the project and ensuring decisions required from the client organization are received in a timely manner. Note that this does not imply the project director should act as a gatekeeper to the project owner – there may be many occasions when the project manager requires direct access to the project owner – but rather that the project director will work with the project manager to meet the project owner's needs.

In general, the project director will manage upwards into the client organization while the project manager manages downwards into the project team. The project director will, however, be responsible for managing the resources the project owner allocates to the project.

The project director will work with both the project owner and project manager in defining the parameters for financial, quality and scheduling control and management of the project, as well as the approach to be taken to the management of risk. Some of these parameters may have already been established by programme management. Where an integrated project team is assembled, the project director and project manager will work together to ensure cohesiveness of the team. The project director will assist the project manager in the resolution of issues and will support, as necessary, the escalation of key issues to the project board. The project director is the first point of contact in the client organization for advisors and contractors and is responsible for ensuring mechanisms are established to encourage good client–contractor relations and manage issues.

The project director will work with the project manager in the development of key project documentation including but not limited to:

- the business case (including in any earlier guise as a preliminary business case);
- the project plan;
- options analysis;
- feasibility studies;
- procurement documentation;
- completion reports, etc.

Skills and attributes of the project director

The project director requires well-developed interpersonal skills, since they will have a significant involvement in stakeholder management and will be dealing with various suppliers to the project, and will also need to develop strong relationships with project owner and senior user client resources. The project director therefore needs to be a good communicator and able to influence others to the extent necessary to gain support for the project among a potentially disparate set of stakeholders. To achieve this will require the ability to network effectively and have a clear understanding of the business needs, drivers and objectives as well as an understanding of the positioning of the project in the broader business environment. These business-facing attributes may need to be learned in the event that the project owner sources the project director from outside the organization.

The project director will need project management skills and will need to understand the project development process. In particular the project director should have competency in the following areas:

- development of a project business case;
- development of the key project documentation likely to be required on the project, including, as required, those listed above;
- understanding of project management methodologies or experience of taking a project from concept through to at least financial close or commencement of construction or build (after this stage in the project the skill set changes and the project director role requires a greater emphasis on contract administration and the technical issues associated with project build or construction in that sector);
- project management techniques and competencies, preferably to the extent detailed in PMBOK (Project Management Institute, 2004);
- risk management;
- procurement options, the circumstances that dictate the selection of specific procurement paths and the implications of taking any particular procurement path;
- tendering processes and tender negotiation techniques.

Project manager

The project manager is not a member of the project board but is included here to indicate the relationship between this role and the project board. Rather than add to the considerable volume of text already devoted to the topic of project management and the role of the project manager, this text reflects on this role only in so far as it relates to the project governance framework.

In respect of the project governance arrangements, the project manager is accountable for delivering the project within the constraints stipulated by the project owner. These constraints are often expressed in terms of time, cost and quality and are specified in various key project documents such as the business case, project plan, business requirements specifications, etc. In doing so, the project manager works closely with the project director, whose role involves ensuring that the project owner's needs, as specified in these documents, are met.

To a varying extent, the project manager will also be held directly accountable within their own organization for delivering that organization's business case. It must always be remembered that the supplier or delivery organization, of which the project manager may be a part, and the project owner or customer's organization have separate and different business cases on any particular project. This is the case even when the project is being delivered by an in-house delivery group. Suppliers will – or should since otherwise their business is at risk – have either an explicit or implicit business case that will guide their approach to the project. There may therefore be an element of tension between the two organizations as a result of this fact. The project manager's performance within their own organization will be measured in part by their delivery of the project owner's business case – ie the extent to which the project owner is satisfied with the service provided by the project manager – and in part by their delivery of the supplier's business case. The project manager is likely to work for the supplier and their remuneration may be linked to the delivery of the supplier's business case – think profit margins. Hence the project director must continue to protect the project owner's interests despite the project manager being charged with delivering the project within the constraints laid down by the project owner in documents such as the business case and project plan. In general terms, major contractual issues can arise when the supplier can no longer deliver the project owner's business case without jeopardizing the supplier's business case.

The project manager supports the project director and project owner at the various meetings as required. This may include attendance at project board, strategic advisors' group and stakeholder working group meetings. The project manager may be employed by the main supplier to the project or may have been separately sourced by the project owner or senior supplier. It is possible that the project manager is a direct report to the senior supplier. Reporting in respect of project decision making is of course through the project board.

The most likely source of confusion regarding roles within the project governance model will be the relationship between the project director and project manager. Both have similar skill sets and work closely together. The project director is concerned with ensuring a successful service delivery outcome and represents the interests of the project owner in this respect. The project manager is generally more concerned with asset delivery. The project manager may not have a contract with the project owner and may work for the chief supplier to the project. This is not to say that a good project manager will not seek to achieve the project owner's service delivery outcomes or that a project director will not have a significant interest in the delivery of the asset. It's just that these will not be their primary focus. Generally, the project director will manage upwards with a strong focus on stakeholder management. The project manager will generally manage downwards into the project.

Executive summary: populating the project governance model

The project owner:

- represents the business;
- is from the organization whose business unit will utilize the outcomes the project delivers;
- has a service delivery focus;
- can't be outsourced.

The senior user:

- represents those who will use the final product or service that the project delivers;

- represents those whom the project may impact in some way, eg operations or maintenance activities;
- may represent an organization that is contributing to funding of the project;
- may be split between two persons if necessary.

The senior supplier:

- represents the suppliers of services to the project;
- may be provided by an in-house service provider or an external provider or both;
- must have the ability to commit supplier resources to the project.

The project director:

- drives the project on behalf of the project owner;
- provides a project delivery skill set to the business;
- manages service delivery outcomes for the project owner.

Case study 2: Introduction of full retail contestability into the English and Welsh electricity market

This case study offers a complex application of the project governance model. It describes the governance of the project as it was delivered and then analyses how it could have been delivered had this project governance model been applied.

Introduction

In 1998 and 1999, full retail contestability was introduced to the electricity market in England and Wales. With its introduction, all households were provided with a choice of electricity supplier. Full retail contestability exists in many electricity markets throughout the world but, in

1998, England and Wales would be the first countries to introduce electricity retail competition at the domestic level at this scale. (Note: Norway, Sweden and Finland opened their market to electricity competition at around the same time.) The trading arrangements and the systems and processes that supported these arrangements were technically complex. In part, this was due to the very nature of electricity. Unlike other commodities such as metals or farm produce, electricity cannot be easily stored in large quantities, so at any point in time the amount of electricity generated must equal the amount of demand in the network. Furthermore, it is not possible to trace any particular quantity of electricity produced by a generator to any particular consumer or even electricity supplier and so the wholesale market for trading electricity between generators and suppliers was based on a pooling arrangement. Generators sell electricity into the 'Pool' and suppliers purchase from the Pool and sell to electricity consumers.

Governance of the Electricity Pool

'The Pool' was the term used to represent the organization of the trading parties in the wholesale market. (Note: The Electricity Pool of England and Wales ceased to be the wholesale market mechanism for trading electricity in England and Wales on 27 March 2001 with the introduction of the New Electricity Trading Arrangements (NETA).) All generators and suppliers participating in the market did so through membership of the Pool as a signatory to the Pooling and Settlement Agreement (PSA), which contained the calculations and the agreements as to how the market was to operate. In particular, the PSA contained the 'Pool Rules' that stipulated the operation of the market. The Pool Rules were themselves supported by a range of agreed procedures and service-level agreements. Together, this suite of documents governed the operation of the market.

Decision making in the Pool was by way of weighted votes according to market share, and since there were in excess of 50 Pool Members, decision making was simplified by the establishment of the Pool Executive Committee. The committee had ten elected representatives, five representing suppliers and five representing generators. It managed the Electricity Pool on behalf of members and was responsible for progressing Pool policy and strategy issues, and overseeing changes to the operation and development of the Pool.

The Pool Executive Committee was supported by the Office of the Chief Executive of the England and Wales Electricity Pool (CEO), which administered the day-to-day business of the Pool. The CEO's work included facilitating the activities of the Pool Executive Committee and its sub-committees by assisting in the overall management of the Pool through routine monitoring of key functions and overall administration of the Pool activities. The Office also assisted with the development of future trading arrangements. The Office was funded by all companies trading in the Electricity Pool and the Chief Executive (known as the Pool CEO) was accountable to Pool Members and the Pool Executive Committee.

Suppliers fell into two groupings: those that were Public Electricity Suppliers (companies that were derived from the original electricity boards), and second-tier suppliers that were new entrants to the market and often associated with generating companies. Until the implementation of the 1998 trading arrangements the bulk of market activity involved the main generators selling into the Pool and the Public Electricity Suppliers buying from the Pool. There was natural tension between the two parties since the general perception was that a 'win' by one group on any particular matter implied a loss by the other. This translated into tension between the Public Electricity Suppliers and second-tier suppliers. Thus, in Pool forums, it was usually necessary to try to balance membership across the two groups.

The 1998 programme

The expansion of competition in electricity supply to all customers brought two main challenges to the Pool. First, the number of customers able to choose their electricity supplier increased from 60,000 to over 23 million. Second, half-hourly settlement of trading was to be based on readings of domestic electricity meters that do not record the electricity used each half-hour period. Thus, systems were required that matched each household to a supplier and estimated the amount of electricity consumption attributed to each supplier on a half-hourly basis, based upon a number of standard usage profiles. It was then possible to calculate on a half-hour by half-hour basis how much electricity each supplier purchased from the pool, and how much money each supplier should pay each generator. This new trading regime was termed the '1998 Trading Arrangements' and was introduced under a programme of work known as the '1998 Programme'.

The 1998 Programme was comprised of a central programme to develop the central systems, processes and commercial arrangements that would enable the market to operate and a number of satellite projects, one for each of the suppliers, to develop the systems and processes they required to operate effectively in the market and interface to the central systems to enable the transfer of metering data and meter readings. The market had many additional technical and commercial complexities in respect of meter operations, data collection and aggregation, supplier default arrangements, agent accreditation, etc that required addressing.

This case study focuses on the central programme of work, which can reasonably be considered as a single project since the constituent projects that comprised the programme were tightly interlinked and independently produced no benefits. Only the coordinated delivery of all projects under the programme could deliver the 1998 Trading Arrangements and, thereby, introduce full retail contestability to the England and Wales electricity market.

The case study has been chosen because of the complex governance issues caused by pooling arrangements, where many parties have a key and central interest in project outcomes and particularly where competitive market tension exists between participants. When this is twinned with the complexity of arrangements required to implement contestability in the England and Wales electricity market it provides a significant challenge for any governance arrangement.

Funding of the programme

Funding for the introduction of the 1998 Trading Arrangements was provided by each supplier market participant. However, the regulator (OFFER) established a cost recovery mechanism whereby companies could recover allowed costs incurred over a specified period of time. Thus, electricity end consumers were effectively funding the 1998 Programme, although their exposure was capped. OFFER allowed the electricity companies £276 million (Green and McDaniel, 1998) for their 1998 programme development costs, although they themselves estimated the cost would be £517 million. The central programme's budget (ie the 1998 Programme) was around £75 million and shared by market participants.

Governance of the 1998 Programme

The governance arrangements of the 1998 Programme are shown diagrammatically in Figure 4.2. Table 4.1 summarizes the 1998 Programme decision-making forums. The functions of the primary bodies and their roles are discussed below. The 1998 Programme was developed using the PRINCE2 project management methodology and much of the following information is taken from the original Programme Initiation Document (PID), which contained detailed terms of reference and responsibility statements for each of the key decision-making roles on the programme.

Programme Steering Group

The Programme Steering Group comprised a total of eight to ten senior individuals representing Pool Members with invitees including OFFER, the Pool Auditor and the Programme Manager. It was chaired by the 1998 Programme Director (see below). The Steering Group was appointed by the Pool Executive Committee and was responsible to it. Their role was to define 'what is required' in terms of the functionality

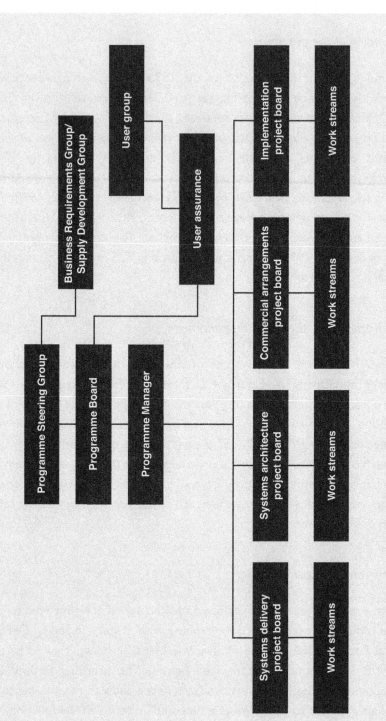

Figure 4.2 1998 Programme governance structure

provided by systems and processes and the commercial arrangements to be employed. In particular, the Programme Steering Group had the following responsibilities:

- appointment of the 1998 Programme Board and the supply development group;
- approval of the terms of reference for the 1998 Programme Board;
- initiation of projects;
- recommend to the Pool Executive Committee approval of changes to the PSA and Pool Rules;
- ensure that all aspects of the requirements for the 1998 Trading Arrangements were implemented;
- administer the funds allocated to the programme by Pool Members;
- authorization of user requirements, specifications and changes to them.

Decisions were reached by a 65 per cent majority of those present and any Pool Member could appeal a decision to the executive committee. The Programme Steering Group met approximately every two weeks.

A member of the steering group approached for this case study remembered their role as dealing with commercial issues arising between members regarding the user and business requirements. In particular issues with serious commercial implications that arose in the Supply Development Group were escalated to the Programme Steering Group. The Steering Group could veto Supply Development Group and Programme Board decisions.

Programme Board

The Programme Board was appointed by the 1998 Programme Steering Group with delegated powers for authorizing expenditure up to an agreed limit. The 1998 Programme board was responsible for delivery of the 1998 Programme to meet the requirements authorized by the 1998 Programme Steering Group and had specific responsibility for:

- authorizing changes to programme plans;
- authorizing project initiation documents;
- appointing project boards;
- ensuring the use of appropriate standards and procedures within the programme team;
- recommending to the 1998 Programme Steering Group acceptance of the 1998 Programme for implementation.

The membership of the programme board comprised two senior users representing suppliers and generators, one senior technical member and was chaired by the 1998 Programme Director. Other invitees included the Programme Manager, senior User Assurance Coordinator and the Pool Auditor. The Programme board met on average every two weeks. There was no voting, and in the event of disagreement the issue in question was referred to the Programme Steering Group. The programme board was to 'discharge the responsibilities of a project board...' under the PRINCE2 methodology.

Programme Director

The Programme Director authorized expenditure items budgeted within the 1998 Programme up to an agreed limit and resolved day-to-day issues raised by the Programme Manager and submission of recommendations to gain subsequent authorization from the Programme Board or Steering Group. The position was held by the CEO of the Electricity Pool. The Programme Director chaired the Programme Steering Group and the Programme Board.

Programme Manager

The Programme Manager was responsible to the Programme Board and Programme Director for managing and delivering the 1998 Programme and reported to the Programme Board. The Programme

Manager was supported by a programme office and a programme team. Individual project managers, reporting to the Programme Manager, were appointed within the team to manage the various projects. The Programme Manager role was outsourced to a specialist IT programme management company. This company led the various projects comprising the programme as well as the programme management office.

Project boards

The project boards were appointed by the 1998 Programme Board with delegated powers for authorizing expenditure up to an agreed limit. The Programme Board appointed project board chairs from among the senior users on the programme board. The project boards were responsible for delivering specific projects to meet the requirements authorized by the 1998 Programme Steering Group. The project boards operated largely in accordance with PRINCE concepts with specific responsibilities that included:

- approving each project initiation document and associated project plan;
- recommending to the Programme Board acceptance of specific projects for implementation;
- enforcing the adoption and the use of the appropriate standards and procedures within the project team.

Each project board comprised three senior members, being one senior user representing suppliers, one representing the generators and one senior technical member. Invitees included the Pool Auditor, User Assurance Coordinator, Assistant Programme Director, Programme Manager and the project manager. Again, there was no voting on decisions. In the event of disagreement, the issue in question was referred to the 1998 Programme Board.

Supply Development Group

The Supply Development Group was formed to resolve business requirements issues. It was appointed by the 1998 Programme Steering Group, to which it reported. Its responsibilities included:

- advising the Programme Steering Group on business requirement issues;
- evaluating business requirement options and recommending preferred options to the Programme Steering Group for approval;
- escalating business requirements issues that it could not resolve to the Programme Steering Group;
- recommending for approval to the Programme Board user requirement specifications, user acceptance criteria and project sign-off;
- recommending the Pool Rules for approval to Pool Members.

The Supply Development Group had representation from all major Pool Members and meetings often comprised in excess of 30 people. It was chaired by the Assistant Programme Director. Gaining agreement of the Supply Development Group to project output could be difficult and time-consuming. Most documents went to the Supply Development Group a minimum of three times – once for initial presentation after it had been issued in advance of the meeting, a second time to indicate how comments that had been received, and were sometimes conflicting, were addressed, and a third time to present the final document. The Supply Development Group met every two weeks.

User group

A user group was appointed to act as a project deliverable review body and to assist the Senior User Assurance Coordinator in resolving programme issues. It had no decision-making authority. It was chaired by the Senior User Assurance Coordinator and comprised Pool Member nominees drawn primarily from the Supply Development Group.

Finally, any supplier could appeal any decision to the regulator, OFFER. Table 4.1 summarizes the key features of the main decision making forums.

Analysis of the 1998 Programme governance arrangements

First and foremost, the 1998 Programme was a success. The central programme of works was delivered on schedule in April 1998, broadly within budget. The supplier systems delivered by the satellite projects were delivered in tranches over the course of the following year. The market worked effectively and all the systems, processes and under-pinning legal and commercial documentation were consistent and comprehensive. There were no significant issues on implementation. This was a major achievement given the complexity of the technical and commercial arrangements and the number of participating organizations.

The challenges associated with the Pool decision-making arrange-ments were largely overcome. The fact of having 50 Pool Members with a collective, albeit weighted, decision-making mechanism had the potential to seriously affect the efficiency of the project decision-making process. That this was largely avoided is noteworthy from a governance perspective and due to a number of factors. First, the timetable for the opening of the domestic market to competition was laid down in legis-lation at the time the market was privatized in 1990. Thus the intro-duction of full retail contestability was an imperative to all the major market participants and was monitored by the regulator, OFFER. Second, the regulator had the authority to resolve issues that threatened to impede or delay market opening. This was an important fallback position as well as an incentive to Pool Members to resolve issues to their mutual satisfaction rather than rely on a ruling from the regulator that may not have been completely desirable to either party. Finally, OFFER also set the window for cost recovery and so delaying market opening risked impacting the ability of the market participants to recover their significant implementation costs.

The analysis will commence with the relationships between the Programme Board, Programme Steering Group and Supply Development

Group. The Programme Board and the Supply Development Group were both established by, and both answered to, the Programme Steering Group. Note also that the chair of the Programme Steering Group and Programme Board was the same – the 1998 Programme Director. Further, the chair of the Supply Development Group was the Assistant Programme Director. Any decision made by either the Supply Development Group or the Programme Board could be overturned by a decision of the Programme Steering Group. This clearly indicates that from a decision-making perspective, the Programme Steering Group was the pre-eminent body in this group. Even decisions of the Programme Steering Group could be overturned by OFFER on appeal. To at least some extent there therefore appears to be an element of serial decision making with the potential for some reduction in decision-making efficiency.

The project boards, being a lower level of decision making again, are of little interest in this analysis. Perhaps, then, the question is whether it would have been possible to remove the elements of serial decision making whilst maintaining the quality of the decision-making process and simultaneously improving efficiency. Could the principles and structures developed in this book have done so?

An alternative approach to the project governance of the 1998 Programme

The challenge is to develop a project governance structure for the 1998 Programme using the principles and approaches described in this book, and in doing so improve the likelihood of efficient and effective decision making.

Selecting the project owner

The 1998 Programme was funded by Pool Members who were either Public Electricity Suppliers or second-tier suppliers. These members were entitled to recover allowed costs over a specified period of time, although the allowed costs were less than the cost of the implementation

Table 4.1 Summary of 1998 Programme decision-making forums

Committee	Programme Steering Group	Programme Board	Supply Development Group
Chair	1998 Programme Director (Pool CEO)	1998 Programme Director (Pool CEO)	Assistant Programme Director (a Director of the Pool CEO's office)
Membership	One voting representative from each Pool Executive Committee member (10 persons)	Three members selected from Pool Members: • Senior User, Public Electricity Suppliers • Senior User, Second-tier Suppliers • Senior technical member • 1998 Development Director	Open to all Pool Members
Invitees	OFFER Representative Pool Auditor Programme Manager + 4 others	Pool Auditor Programme Manager + 4 others	OFFER Representative Pool Auditor Programme Manager + others
Approximate number of attendees	18	10	20 to 40
Decision making	Voting, 65% majority	Consensus	Consensus
Issue escalation	OFFER	Programme Steering Group	Programme Steering Group
Key responsibilities	Appoints and approves the terms of reference of 1998 Programme Board Authorizes changes to the Pool Rules and other procedures Recommends to Pool Executive Committee approval of changes to the Pooling and Settlement Agreement Ensures all aspects of the 1998 Trading Arrangements are implemented	Authorizes Programme and Project Initiation Documents Recommends, to 1998 Steering Group, acceptance of the 1998 Programme for implementation Enforces appropriate standards and procedures within Programme Team Authorizes changes to Programme Plan	Advises Programme Steering Group on business requirement issues Recommends preferred business requirement options to Programme Steering Group for approval Escalates unresolved business requirements issues to Programme Steering Group Recommends user documentation to 1998 Programme Board for approval

as estimated by the suppliers. It can therefore be argued that, from the funding perspective, the project owner should be drawn from the ranks of suppliers. The retailing of electricity to consumers is a service that rests squarely with the suppliers, as does the realization of the project's benefits. Even though it could be argued that Public Electricity Suppliers had little incentive to introduce competition that removed their monopoly and therefore did not fit the classic mould of a project owner who seeks to gain benefits from a project, second-tier suppliers would benefit from the project and the more aggressive of the Public Electricity Suppliers also sought to gain from competition.

If the project owner is to be drawn from the ranks of suppliers, the logical choice is the 1998 Programme Director who is also the Pool CEO. This person is appointed by and answerable to Pool Members and as such is a logical choice as project owner. It was also clear that the Pool CEO was considered accountable for the implementation of the new trading arrangements. One issue that arises is the appeals process run by OFFER, which could conceivably overturn a project owner decision. This is not ideal, but then it could be argued that OFFER holds this position not just in respect of the programme but in respect of the overall operation of the market.

Hence the 1998 Programme board will be formed around the chief Executive of the Electricity Pool as the project owner.

Other project board roles

The senior user role is relatively straightforward and could be filled by two Pool members, selected from the Pool Executive Committee, with one representing Public Electricity Suppliers and the other second-tier suppliers. The senior supplier role will require a representative of the main consultancy advisor chosen to manage the programme.

A project of this complexity requires a full-time project director. Remember that the project director acts for the project owner and is that person's representative on the project, ensuring the project remains focused at all times on the business need and service delivery outcome. The project director also provides project management skills that may not be part of the project owner's skill set. In many respects, the Assistant Programme Director who was a direct report of the Pool Chief Executive, acted as a de facto project director on the 1998 Programme. Note also that this person chaired the Supply Development Group and fully understood the complexity of the programme. It therefore makes sense for the person who acted in this role to fill the project director role.

The programme manager reports to this new project board. The programme manager effectively maps to the role that our standard governance structure refers to as project manager – remember that although referred to as a programme, the projects that comprise the 1998 Programme are so tightly interlinked as to be considered work streams of a single project. Although the work streams that were led by the individual project boards are a key work management tool, the individual project boards themselves did not have the authority to make binding decisions, since they could be overruled by the Programme Board or Programme Steering Group. Whilst a leadership cohort was essential for each work stream, it is proposed that these not be referred to as project boards to avoid confusion and to reflect the fact that they are an internal project management tool rather than a part of this alternative governance arrangement.

The governance structure at this point in our alternative redesign is represented in Figure 4.3. Note that where the new role is filled by a designated role from the original governance arrangements, it is shown with an = sign.

The investment decision group

The issue of how to address the investment decision group is an interesting one. There was no question that the introduction of electricity competition would proceed, and therefore in some respects the investment decision had effectively been made by the government. Suppliers of course determined the extent of the investment required.

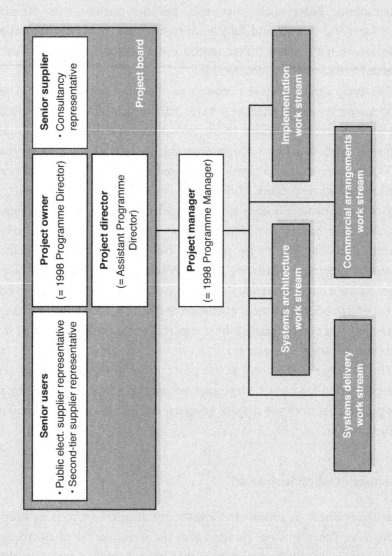

Figure 4.3 1998 Programme alternative governance structure – stage 1

In circumstances where governments announce projects this is not an unusual situation, but it does not necessarily imply that there is no role for an investment decision group. For instance, the key document that defines the project and its costs and benefits is the project's business case. Even when the investment decision has been previously made, there remains significant value in developing the business case to ensure clarity of objectives, agreement on critical success factors, alignment of stakeholders, understanding of the costs and benefits and so on. The investment decision group requires the business case because it defines exactly what it is that the funding parties are agreeing to fund. Eliminating this step is not recommended.

However, in this situation, there are multiple funding parties and no one organization or party fulfilling the role of investment custodian – in fact there are in excess of 50 funding bodies, as well as OFFER in its role as consumer guardian and owner of the cost recovery mechanism. The Public Electricity Suppliers and second-tier suppliers are represented in the new project board, although OFFER is not. It would be up to the project owner to decide whether OFFER should be an invitee to project board meetings, although the answer, in retrospect, is probably 'yes'. An investment decision group would simply mirror this group and it is therefore proposed that in this special case no investment decision group be constituted – or rather that the alternative project board act also as the investment decision group. This arrangement implies delegated financial authority be granted to members of the alternative project board by the organizations they represent.

Completing the revised 1998 Programme project governance framework

The strategic advisors group needs to contain either the key project stakeholders outside of the project board or their representatives. The existing Programme Steering Group contains the necessary representation to meet this requirement. It has one representative from each of the ten Pool Executive Committee members, along with representatives from OFFER, the Pool Auditor and others. The Pool Members providing the senior user positions on the project board would not need representation here as well, thereby allowing other Pool Members to take their place on the strategic advisors' group. In the event that other Pool Members insisted on a place at the strategic advisors' group, they could be accommodated; however, its membership is already around 18 and further expansion would be unwise.

The stakeholder working group is also already constituted in the form of the Supply Development Group. The detailed activity this group undertook on the 1998 Programme makes them ideally suited for this role. The user group and user assurance function can remain as is and in any case play only a supporting role in decision making – they are therefore not shown on the revised arrangements. The final revised project governance framework is shown in Figure 4.4.

Conclusion

The 1998 Programme represents a very stringent test of this project governance framework. The suggested arrangements are somewhat simpler than those they would replace and that in itself should be an advantage. The main question therefore is whether any value is being lost through the simplification. The new arrangements would require more decision making to be devolved to the work streams, thereby compensating for the replacement of the 1998 Programme Board and Steering Committee by the project board alone. However, issues can still be resolved by the stakeholder working group (the old Supply Development Group) and at the strategic advisors' group (the old Programme Steering Group).

While the number of committees has not been reduced – there remain three – there have been two significant changes: the number of key decision-making bodies has been reduced from three excluding work streams, to one – the project board; and the number of people involved in direct decision making as opposed to advisory roles has been reduced from over 50 to 5, with no loss in terms of the quality of input received.

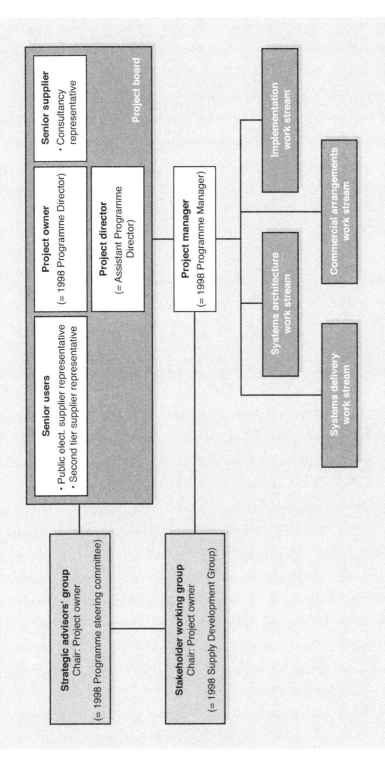

Figure 4.4 1998 Programme alternative governance structure

5 Scalability

This book presents an ideal project governance framework consisting of the four principles of effective project governance, the project governance model and the associated advice regarding the model's constituents. Following this framework will provide a high degree of confidence that a project's governance arrangements will be satisfactorily addressed.

The project governance model itself is specifically designed to address the needs of high-risk projects. After all, the model would lack credibility and usefulness were it not able to deal with such projects. The more complex and riskier the project, the more likely that all elements of the model will be required to adequately address that risk. By implication, then, there may be opportunities for lower-risk projects to flex or scale the model without losing its intent or the benefits it delivers. There are two main drivers for scaling back the project governance model:

- The first is to ease the overhead on less complex projects. Not every project will require all the elements of the model we have developed, and in particular circumstances it may be prudent to simplify, adjust or augment the project governance model to meet particular needs, requirements or imposed constraints.
- Second, there may be certain circumstances where it becomes necessary to make compromises when developing the project governance

arrangements for any particular project, especially those at the high end of the risk spectrum. This can occur when organizational politics enters the equation. Projects may come under pressure to add to or subtract stakeholders from the project governance arrangements as a result of either internal or external politicking. In some instances this may be unavoidable and so the project governance arrangements are compromised to some extent.

If it is to be possible to alter the model without damaging the project, it is necessary to know two things: 1) what risk level is associated with any particular project, since this will be one indication of the extent to which it is prudent to relax the project governance model; and 2) to what extent the project governance model can be flexed without losing its effectiveness.

Assessing project risk

What is of interest here is an overall assessment of the riskiness of the project to the organization. This needs to be determined quite early in the project's development if it is to feed into decisions around the project's governance arrangements and be broad enough to capture all main risk areas. In the absence of detailed information to feed into a risk assessment at this early stage in the project, organizations often use the project's expected capital cost as a proxy for risk – the higher the capital cost, the greater the risk associated with that project. While there is some logic to this it is not recommended, particularly as a better solution is achievable. The problems associated with using capital cost as a proxy for risk include:

- While there may be little knowledge of project risk at this early stage in the project's development, there is also little understanding of the likely capital cost of the project either. To compound this problem is the ever-present issue of optimism bias, whereby organizations tend to have a more optimistic outlook on the expected cost of a project than the organization's history of delivery of such projects would warrant.
- An initial focus on the capital cost of a project is not an overly healthy approach to project delivery. As has been discussed, the project

owner must take a whole-of-life perspective since the project is, for them, enabling a service outcome. A capital cost focus is at odds with this approach.

- A capital cost proxy for risk may give a false impression of the level of risk facing the project. For example, when costing ICT projects, organizations often do not capitalize or even address the business change costs of the implementation of new systems, thereby artificially suppressing the project's capital cost. Yet business change is one of the greatest risk areas facing ICT projects. What then appears to be a relatively low capital cost implementation can easily contain high elements of risk for the organization, out of proportion to the capital cost of the system asset being delivered.
- And finally, the opposite can also occur, where projects with relatively high capital cost have quite low risk profiles.

A more accurate measure of project risk than capital cost is therefore desirable. This issue has been addressed by others also seeking a measure of the inherent risk faced by a project. The Office of Government Commerce in the United Kingdom faced this very problem when having to identify the project risk levels for application of the OGC Gateway™ Process. They developed a risk potential assessment that provides a fairly broad indication of the level of risk associated with the project, based upon factors such as the experience of the organization in dealing with projects of that nature, the extent of proven technology used in the solution, the experience of the project team, and so on (OGC, undated b). More detail on the potential contents of such a risk assessment tool is provided in the text box below.

Project risk profile model

The following provides the main risk categories that a project risk profile model could include. Note that not all the data may be known at the very start of the project and some may have to be estimated. Potential risk categories include:

- the experience of key personnel of delivery of this type of project;
- market maturity in delivering this type of project;
- availability of resources;

- the visibility of the project to the community (primarily government projects);
- the importance of the project to the organization;
- capital and whole-of-life costs;
- value of expected benefits;
- number of staff affected;
- impacts on other parts of the organization or other organizations;
- the extent to which the project involves business and process change;
- the maturity of the technology being used;
- whether the project is green field or brown field;
- for ICT projects, the extent of integration with other systems.

Each category can be scored and weighted, resulting in an overall risk score for a project.

Such models aren't intended to be comprehensive; they simply provide an initial view of the potential risk level associated with a project and have the added benefit of providing an early focus on project risk. Using such tools, the organization can develop a broad potential risk ranking of projects in the delivery pipeline. This can be used to arrive at a view as to what level of governance is suitable for any particular project.

The limits of scalability

The next step is to determine the extent to which the project governance model may be scaled without its effectiveness being compromised. This requires a knowledge of where ground can be given and where giving ground could compromise the integrity of the governance arrangements. Our first step then is to determine those limits which, when exceeded, compromise the effectiveness of the project governance arrangements – in other words, where to draw the line. This discussion is best conducted by reference to the core principles of project governance, restated in the text box below.

The four principles of effective project governance

1. Ensure a single point of accountability for the success of the project.
2. Service delivery ownership determines project ownership.
3. Ensure separation of stakeholder management and project decision-making activities.
4. Ensure separation of project governance and organizational governance structures.

The concept of a single point of accountability is immutable. Accountability for the success of the project cannot be split; two people cannot be accountable for the success of a project. The outcome, if this is attempted, is likely to be a blurring of accountability and reduced decision-making effectiveness. Therefore, there must always be a single person identified as accountable for the success of a project.

The second principle is concerned with where that person sits within the organization. It has been previously stated that ownership of the project must lie with the person or organizational role who must live with the outcome the project delivers. The simplest way of viewing this concept is to conceptualize projects as platforms for delivering services. Ownership of the service therefore defines ownership of the project. Is it possible to move away from that concept for low(er)-risk projects? For instance, is it feasible to transfer accountability for the success of a low-risk project to the project manager? This may appear quite an attractive option for a hard-pressed project owner with more complex and higher-risk projects to deliver. The simple answer is 'no'. The business must always own the project, and unless the project manager is part of the business – part of the organization or that group within it responsible for delivering the core service – this will not be the case. What can work is the arrangement whereby the project owner takes on the additional role of the project manager, assuming they have the skills and time to do so.

Therefore, not only is it necessary to maintain a single point of accountability, the project owner must always represent the business and thereby maintain the governance focus on delivery of a service rather than it being primarily focused on the delivery of an asset. By implication, the project owner must be an employee of the organization – outsourcing of the project owner role is never an option. Hence, the second principle is also immutable.

Principle 3 is concerned with the efficiency and effectiveness of project decision making. If stakeholder management and project decision making are not separated the most obvious outcome will be a swelling of numbers in project board meetings. This will make the meetings less effective and is likely to damage the decision-making effectiveness of the project board. The larger the project board, the more likely its decision-making effectiveness will be impaired. There is no specific cut-off point at which the transition from effective to ineffective decision making occurs. However, practice has shown that six people appear to offer the necessary flexibility in terms of ensuring an effective and representative project board. The key message therefore is to keep as close as possible to six (or fewer) people on the project board, since the further away one moves, the less effective and efficient the project decision-making capability of the group is likely to be.

Principle 4 can be treated similarly. This principle is in part aimed at ensuring the project board does not lose its authority through having its decisions ratified by the organization chain of command. Invariably this involves 'inserting' the project board into the organization structure, thereby creating a hybrid project governance structure/organization structure. As for Principle 3, the effect of this principle is to increase the effectiveness and efficiency of the decision-making process, and the further the project moves from this principle the less effective and efficient the project decision-making process will become. When faced with this situation, where the project board is under pressure to have its decisions ratified by the organization's chain of command, there are two options. Either the concerns and interests of those within the chain of command can be accommodated by their membership of the strategic advisors' group, which is the obvious and most likely route, or, alternatively, stronger, perhaps one-on-one reporting can be employed. Often the driver for executives to want to ratify project board decisions is not so much control as information. Providing they have up-to-date project information that meets their needs, their requirement for actual control is diminished. A consideration in relaxing this principle is that ratification of project board decisions implies a lessening of the necessary authority of the project owner, which consequently has an impact on their accountability.

Main scalability options

The above provides guidelines for consideration when scaling back the project governance framework. This section explores how the project governance arrangements can be scaled to accommodate projects with lower risk profiles. The project governance model is reproduced for convenience in Figure 5.1.

The first point to make is that when modifying the project governance model the intention is not to lose or discard roles, but rather to combine them with other roles where this is appropriate. The individual project board roles are generally required on all projects, regardless of the level of complexity. So, for instance, all projects have a business/project owner, users, and a supplier. The role of the project director is an exception to this rule and could be discarded in a project of lower complexity since it is primarily a supporting role to that of the project owner. Similarly, all projects have a project manager and stakeholders, and involve an investment decision.

Referring to Figure 5.1, as the project complexity decreases, the project governance model can gradually be scaled back in broadly the following manner. The exact nature of the scaling that is employed is of course dependent on the project itself, the organization and the prevailing circumstances.

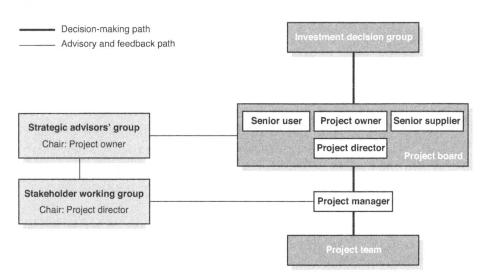

Figure 5.1   The project governance model

- The stakeholder working group consists of technical stakeholders who, in their own organizations, generally report to those stakeholders in the strategic advisors' group. In less complex projects, the stakeholder working group could be subsumed within the strategic advisors' group.
- The project director is there to support the project owner. This role reflects the fact that the project owner may not have the necessary time available to commit to the project because of the considerable day-to-day responsibilities of the position they hold within the organization. Further, large and complex projects require strong project management credentials on the business side of the project as well as the delivery side, and not all project owners will have this skill set. Projects of lower complexity may not require the support the project director provides to the project owner, and so for lower-risk projects this role may prove less important.
- All projects have users and on that basis the role of senior user is always required. The project owner, as the business owner of the project, will always have an interest in ensuring the needs of users are met since this will, in part, determine the success of the project. Where the needs of users are closely aligned with the business requirements of the project owner, it is possible the project owner could also assume the role of senior user. The danger in pursuing this course is that the needs of users will not be adequately met and this approach should not be dictated by a lack of project resources.
- The strategic advisors' group contains those stakeholders whose actions can either prove of support to the project or, alternatively, can do the project harm. The reason for forming them into a single group is so that they can be managed more efficiently. The formation of the strategic advisors' group does not obviate the need for the project owner to work closely with key stakeholders outside of this forum. In the event that the number of key stakeholders associated with a project is small, there may be no good reason to assemble this group. Instead the project owner and project director would continue to work with the stakeholders on a one-to-one basis.

It is relatively straightforward to envisage relaxations to the formal project governance model beyond those discussed above; however, this moves into the realm of quite low-risk projects. For instance, a very low-risk project could support the project owner taking the role of project manager and, with the correct delegated authority in place, even the role of the investment decision group.

Executive summary: Scalability options for lower-risk projects

Scalability considerations for the four principles of effective project governance:

1. Must maintain single point of accountability.
2. Business must always own the project.
3. Try to avoid including more than six people on the project board.
4. Try to avoid ratification of project board decisions by the organization.

Scalability considerations for the project governance model:

- combine roles rather than discard them;
- the strategic advisors' group takes on stakeholder working group activity;
- the project owner fulfils the project director role;
- the project owner assumes the senior user role;
- project owner/project director briefings replace the strategic advisors' group.

6 Implementing the project governance framework

Implementing change

The implementation of this project governance framework across an organization is an exercise in business change management. The fact that the framework is articulated in this text is helpful but does not obviate the need to take a change management approach to its roll-out within an organization. The project governance framework is a management process, concerned as it is with decision making, and its implementation will require the same care towards ensuring its acceptance as does any new process. To ignore this requirement risks failure of the implementation. This section investigates approaches and techniques that may assist the implementation of this project governance framework and investigates the issues that may arise and means of overcoming them. It is not intended to be a fully comprehensive approach to the management of change. It also includes an implementation case study.

Establishing the need

A successful implementation requires that the organization and its executives are convinced of the need for either new or revised project governance arrangements. One of the difficulties in implementing a framework such as this is that the need is not always apparent. While it may be obvious within an organization that the quality of their project delivery is not as good as it should be, it may not be obvious that a fundamental element of the problem is ineffective project governance. Hence it is important to first establish the need for new project governance arrangements in the organization before commencing on the implementation path, and there are a number of ways of doing this.

If the organization has existing project governance policies and procedures, the first step is to obtain a clear understanding of how these operate. Of course, these existing policies may be quite effective and require only fine tuning. If they are not, this needs to be made apparent to the organization. One approach that has been used successfully is to map the existing arrangements, showing the relationships between the various bodies and roles referenced by the policy document(s), indicating which documents are signed off by which authorities, what paths the various key project documents take for approval and so forth. An example of this approach is provided in Figure 6.1.

Each element on the map is referenced to the section of the policy or procedure from which it was derived. The benefit of this visual mapping is that it will normally become quickly apparent if the organization's project governance arrangements are flawed. For instance, it is not possible to view the arrangements in Figure 6.1 as anything other than flawed.

The next step, or, if the organization has no project governance policy, the starting point, becomes the four principles of effective project governance. Most people with an understanding of projects relate quickly to the principles – they understand the reasoning behind them and recognize that they address issues that in the past have had a negative impact on projects with which they have had an involvement. Hence from a change management perspective, the benefit of the principles is that it is unlikely there will be any significant objection to their adoption. The principles can be used as a baseline, comparing existing practice to them and indicating where existing practice could be improved. They also act as a staging post towards adoption of the overall framework,

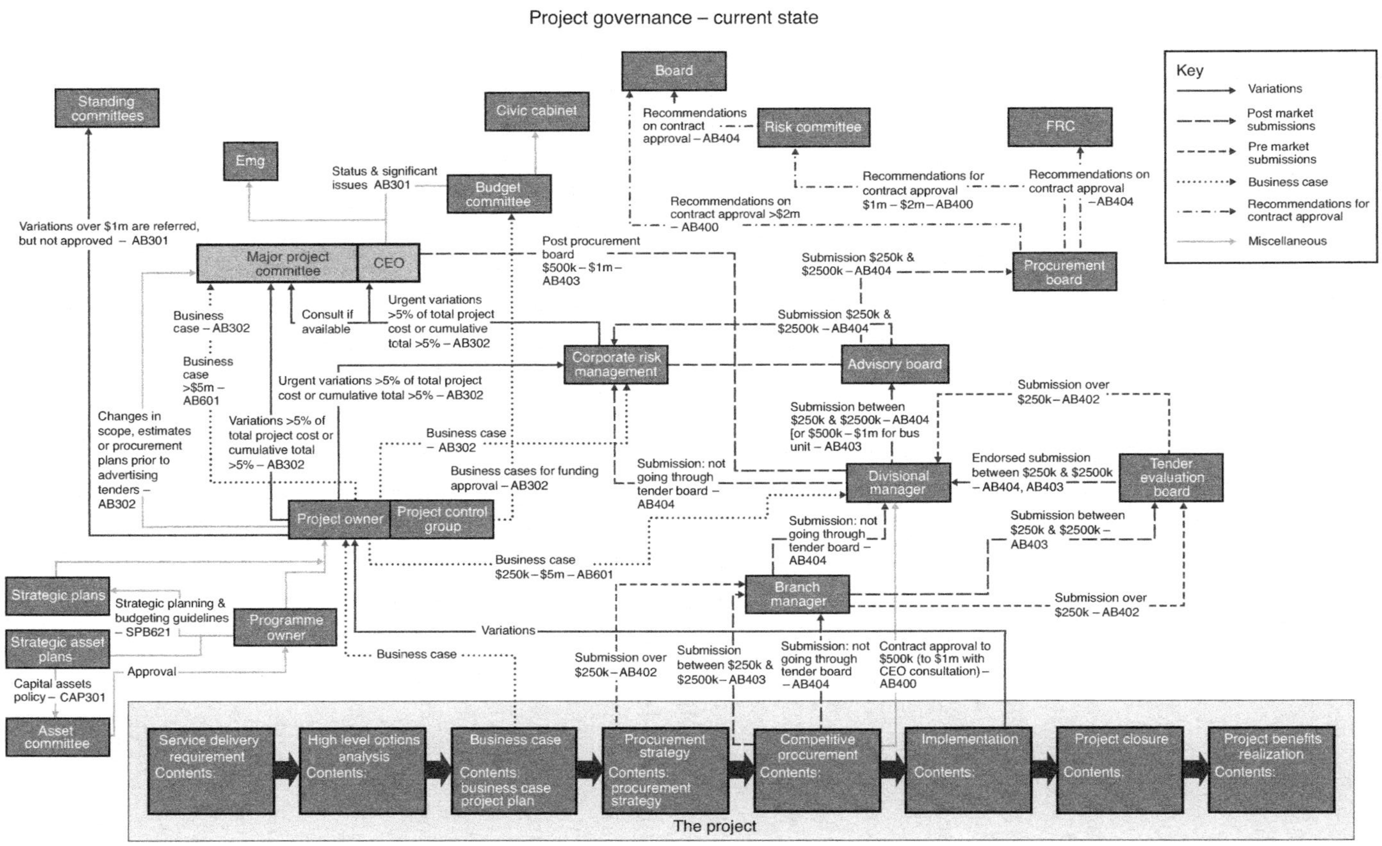

Figure 6.1 Example of a governance map

Note: internal divisional checks and approvals are not shown. References [eg AB404] are to policies and procedures

which otherwise requires a certain level of faith before its fundamentals are fully understood. The combination of the mapping of existing policy and procedures and the comparison of existing practice with the four principles of effective project governance should be sufficient to establish the need for change.

Senior management commitment

The importance of ensuring senior management support cannot be over-stated, despite it being a virtual cliché. The sooner in the implementation of this project governance framework that this can be achieved, the easier the implementation will be. Management support is important for a number of reasons that become very apparent once the framework is in place. The project board must have the necessary authority to ensure its decisions are accepted by the organization's top management without the need for further ratification. Remember that a fundamental reason for establishing a project board is to separate the governance of the project from the organization's structure. If project board decisions require rati-fication by line management within the organization structure then this has not been achieved. Hence the need for management to sign up to the principles and framework of the new project governance arrangements. Note too that the project board, or at least the project owner, may require delegated authority under the project governance policy. Thus certain organizational policy changes may be necessary.

A further driver for obtaining top management support is in estab-lishing the importance of the strategic advisors' group. There may be a tendency for senior management to want a seat on the project board rather than in the strategic advisors' group, since the former is the project's decision-making body, whereas the latter is primarily an advisory body. The reality is that senior stakeholders will have considerable influence on the project irrespective of where they sit. If an important stakeholder is better placed in the strategic advisors group than on the project board, this is unlikely to diminish their influence on the project. Senior management will need to buy in to the importance of the strategic advisors' group since they may find their involvement on some projects channelled through this route. It will be helpful if senior management show leadership in this area by nominating themselves or direct reports for strategic advisors' group membership on projects. This is particularly the case for central agencies in government or corporate/head office functions in the private sector (eg prime minister/premier's office, treasury and finance, centralized centres of excellence, corporate services, corporate risk management, etc). This is because they often have a strong generic interest in many projects but do not fit the role of project owner, senior user or senior supplier on any particular project. The exception of course is 'whole of corporation' initiatives where the project owner may be right-fully drawn from these areas. Generally speaking, though, there is almost a tradition in governance arrangements to include representatives of these senior corporate groups in the steering committees or other decision-making bodies of major projects when, as this governance framework has shown, their rightful place is as strategic advisors. It therefore sends a strong message if senior management in the organization nominate them-selves for inclusion in the strategic advisors' group of specific projects rather than to the project board.

One possible impact of this project governance framework is that it will place a greater emphasis on the service delivery side of the business in delivering projects than was previously the case. The focal point of project delivery, and certainly of project governance, may subtly shift from the project management side of the organization to the business or service delivery side. This change needs to be managed because in the delivery of projects neither side of the business can deliver without the other. Thus, at senior management levels, there needs to be a clear understanding of this partnership and how it will work in practice.

Gaining support in the organization

Once top management are supportive of the need to implement new project governance arrangements, the next task is to gain support for the arrangements throughout the organization at the officer level. It's unrealistic to expect any changes to be welcomed immediately and so it is necessary to plan their implementation. Even if the implementation is mandated by executive management, the reality is that unless relevant officers throughout the organization are supportive, it won't be fully effective. Without entering too deeply into the realm of business change management, the following are some techniques that have been used to good effect in various business environments.

- User or reference groups can be used as a means of rolling out a new concept. Once such a group is established, it is of course necessary to act on any concerns or issues they raise. This in turn involves providing them with the opportunity to say what they don't like about the new arrangements, and it is certain there will be issues. Since the project governance arrangements described herein are logical, simple and robust, overcoming issues should not be difficult. The user group should comprise both project owners and those from the project delivery side of the organization, including project managers. If the organization has a programme office they too should be represented in the group.

Overcoming issues – one approach

On one occasion when I was implementing this framework, I had established a user group and it was clear they had many issues they wanted addressing, not all of which a project governance framework would be able to resolve. I was therefore anticipating issues when I unveiled the proposed project governance model, even though by this stage they had agreed to the four principles of effective project governance.

To address their concerns I projected the structure onto a wall and we spent the meeting applying Post-it Notes to it, to indicate their general concerns with the arrangements. Each person had the opportunity to address their concerns with the group. The meeting ended with my undertaking to address all the concerns and provide a response to each. We then agreed we would discuss this at next meeting and agree on the way forward. The comments broadly fell into two categories: those that could be addressed by further explanation of the project governance framework and how it would be applied, and those that no project governance arrangement was ever going to be able to resolve and were generally issues specific to that organization and its culture.

Once their project governance concerns were addressed through further explanation, and those that couldn't be resolved by the project governance framework put to one side, the initial resistance to the arrangements largely fell away. By the next meeting they had had a month to become familiar with the new project governance arrangements, which had therefore ceased to be new and threatening. They also had the confidence of knowing that, through their ongoing involvement in the user group, they would have input and control over the development of the new arrangements.

- The approach of piloting a number of projects can also reduce initial resistance as well as iron out issues associated with the implementation. It is best to choose a range of pilots across different project types to avoid the 'but we're different' syndrome.
- Trial periods can be useful to overcome concerns. State that the new arrangements will be implemented on a 12-month trial basis and the situation reassessed at the end of that time. This is useful in ironing out teething problems as well as providing a low-key implementation of the new arrangements. The user group can be maintained during this period to provide feedback and raise issues.

The challenges of implementing the project governance framework

Implementing the project governance framework may result in significant changes to the way an organization delivers projects and those changes will have associated issues. This section addresses some of the main issues an organization is likely to encounter when implementing this project governance framework.

Cultural issues

The implementation of new project governance arrangements may involve cultural change within an organization. The extent of this will be dependent on the organization itself. Traditionally, project delivery has been the remit of project managers who have viewed themselves as the drivers of projects. The new arrangements emphasize the early developmental stages of a project and ensure that the overall development of the project is being driven by the project owner and therefore the service delivery arm of the business. This may be perceived as a loss of power or influence by the project management or delivery side of the business, compounded by the perception that the service delivery arm has little knowledge of project delivery – a perception that may well be true. The true situation is that this project governance framework benefits both parties – project management and service delivery. Without a strong project owner focus on the project, the project management or delivery arm of the organization must second-guess what the business needs and, as they are focused on asset delivery, they may not be able to draw out from the business the true service delivery needs. In any case, it is not necessarily their responsibility. The message therefore is not one of reducing the power or influence of the project management area of the organization but rather of increasing the sophistication of the business to better fulfil their role in project delivery. This is a win–win relationship since neither party can truly excel without the other. The new project governance arrangements strengthen the relationship and ensure project delivery occurs as a seamless activity throughout the project's lifecycle, rather than being one in which the business passes an ill-defined brief to the project managers and waits to see what comes back.

Although it may seem obvious, it may be necessary to make the point that the structure depicted in the project governance model does not indicate organizational chain of command relationships. In other words, senior supplier resources in the project team are not direct reports to the project owner in the organizational sense. The model is a project governance model, not an organizational model and shows decision making and advisory relationships in respect of a project. For example, if the project manager and the senior supplier are from the same organization, it is quite possible the project manager reports to the senior supplier in that organization. This project governance model does not alter that relationship. Therefore the project manager in such circumstances is likely to take direction from the senior supplier on the project. Key project decisions, however, are made via the project board and must be agreed by the project owner because it is their project. For further clarity on this point, refer to the section on operationalizing the project governance framework (page 118).

An organization may also resist the need to delegate the necessary authority to the project board. In part this may be driven by a concern that delegation of authority may result in a lack of information being received about the project; prior to the introduction of these project governance arrangements, executives may well have received project updates through membership of large and cumbersome steering committees – a reasonable way to obtain information but not to make decisions. An executive who finds that not only are they no longer a member of the new project board but are being asked to delegate certain authority to that board may have legitimate concerns around the extent to which their future project-information needs will be met. Executives' concerns in this respect are reasonable since their superiors may well expect them to have sufficient understanding of the project to be able to provide briefs. This serves to re-emphasize the point made much earlier in this book that these project governance arrangements do not address or replace the need for reporting requirements. Any executive with project information needs who is not a member of the project board, strategic advisors group or stakeholder working group will need to receive regular reports on the project's progress and the issues it faces. The better the quality of infor-mation an executive is provided on a project, the more likely they are to relinquish control and delegate to the project owner/project board.

Of course there may also be an issue around delegation in that officers may not wish to accept accountability for the success of a project. Depending on the culture of the organization, accountability may be a very daunting mantle to assume. Clearly, organizations that have a 'blame' culture may face a lack of desire among the service delivery personnel to assume the role of project owner. The importance of accountability to this project governance framework is due to the empow-erment it provides to the project owner and the authority the project owner has to make key decisions. Its importance has nothing to do with 'finger-pointing' in the event the project is less than successful. The organization must accept that project officers at all levels will do their best to ensure project success but that failures do occur. General experience has been that service delivery officers are very keen to assume project owner roles because it provides them with the necessary authority and control to deliver projects that meet their service delivery needs.

Corporate policy issues

An organization should have a clear, high-level vision and goals that cascade down through strategies and programmes and finally to indi-vidual projects. If an organization lacks any of these strategic levels, indi-vidual projects will be forced to make their own assumptions to fill the vacuum. This runs the risk that different projects take different strategic directions or can result in project outcomes that are not aligned with the organization's goals. Alternatively, projects are delayed whilst executive management make decisions on matters of policy raised by the project. Strong project governance arrangements can highlight shortcomings in an organization's policy and strategic framework. By releasing the decision-making 'log jam' at the project level, project governance may identify issues in other areas of the organization.

Procurement policy can become an issue for the project owner and project board when 'unwritten rules' exist. This may occur when organizations have in-house delivery arms that, for whatever reason, do not have good relationships with the business or have questionable delivery track records. In these circumstances, the project owner may well wish to consider external procurement options. If the organization, however, has an 'understanding' that work must first be offered to the internal provider, then the project owner's preferred option will be overruled. This introduces issues around the project owner's accountability. It is best for the organization to have a clear policy in this respect, although that may of course raise other issues.

Structural issues

This is an area that has been mentioned previously and concerns the alignment of the project owner, the service delivery arm of the business and the project budget. The project owner must represent that area of the organization responsible for service delivery. Budget responsibility must also rest in this area. Restating the logic of this position, the person who owns the budget owns the project on which the budget is being spent and, therefore, the outcome the project delivers. Thus there is a continuous link between project owner, the budget and service delivery. However, significant organizational changes such as major reorganizations or restructures can result in misalignment – for instance the budget not residing with the service delivery arm of the business or project ownership being vested in the asset delivery areas of the business. Either situation will create significant difficulty for the organization in project delivery.

The ICT sector is one area where misalignment sometimes occurs. There can sometimes be a tendency for the project ownership of ICT-enabled business change to reside with an organization's ICT group. Since the latter is a delivery arm of the organization rather than a core business unit, this is unlikely to result in fully successful outcomes. The business must retain ownership of the project.

Resourcing and skills issues

The major resourcing impacts resulting from the implementation of these project governance arrangements are felt by the service delivery area within the organization. Generally speaking, project delivery or supplier resources are not impacted since project managers and their teams are largely unaffected. The impact is felt mainly by the project owner and senior user, who need to bring business resources to the project to define and monitor the delivery of their requirements. Further, the point has been made earlier that when faced with an increased capital works programme, organizations tend in any case to concentrate project resourcing effort on the project management area, while sometimes ignoring the resourcing needs of the service delivery/business arm.

In the earliest phases of the project, the project owner has the task of ensuring strategic alignment of the project with the organization's goals and vision, defining the project's drivers, objectives, benefits, critical success factors and so on. To do this effectively requires business resources dedicated to the project. The business must then monitor the project's development to ensure service delivery continues to be the focus. The project owner will do well to ensure that dedicated business resources are in place to undertake this activity on their behalf. The quality of decision making on a project is dependent upon the quality of the information upon which the decisions are made, and while the project owner and project director can rely to a large extent upon information provided by the project manager and project team, greater assurance will be obtained with business resources dedicated to the project and its service delivery aims.

These project governance arrangements clearly place an additional burden on project owners. While the framework supports them with project directors, this nevertheless constitutes a significant impact on their workload. In the following section we investigate methods that help to reduce this load. The ideal approach for an organization that is consistently delivering projects is to accept the fact that the delivery of projects is a core function and staff the business accordingly to meet this workload. In doing so it is important not to lose sight of the fact that it is business resources that are needed. The benefit will be lost if all that is created is a new or expanded project delivery group. One indicator that business resourcing needs to address is that when upon listing the projects to be delivered, the same names consistently emerge as project owner and/or project director.

When an organization acts to increase the number of potential project owners and project directors it must remember that while project director roles can be contracted in for the duration of the project, this is unwise when sourcing project owners. Project owners should always be core business personnel. To outsource this role is to outsource core business. As previously discussed, it is not always essential for the project owner to have project delivery skills. In some sectors, it is quite likely that they will. These are typically engineering-focused organizations such as government roads and transport departments or private sector organizations with a predominantly engineering focus such as the resources sector. Other sectors may have to accept that the operational skill set and project delivery skill sets are very different and it will be difficult to have both skill sets fulfilled by the same person. In circumstances such as this, the choice of project director becomes critical since they may be providing many project delivery skills missing from the project owner's repertoire. The ICT sector often typifies this issue where there may be a considerable gap between the skills of the business executive and the skill set necessary to deliver an ICT-enabled business change.

The senior user is responsible for procuring user resources for the project. Again, as for owner resources, the business will be required to provide the bulk of these resources. It is difficult to envisage user resources being contracted in, since those who represent the interests of users must themselves have a very clear understanding of user operations and this will not be achieved with outsourced resources. The following section provides various opportunities for overcoming resourcing issues and operationalizing the project governance arrangements in your organization.

Operationalizing the project governance framework

Figure 6.2 investigates the resourcing associated with a project from the perspective of the project board members. It indicates for each member the resources they are likely to be managing as part of an integrated project team.

Referring to the figure, the project owner potentially has a range of resources to call upon to assist them in delivering the project. First and foremost is the project director, who manages the project owner's

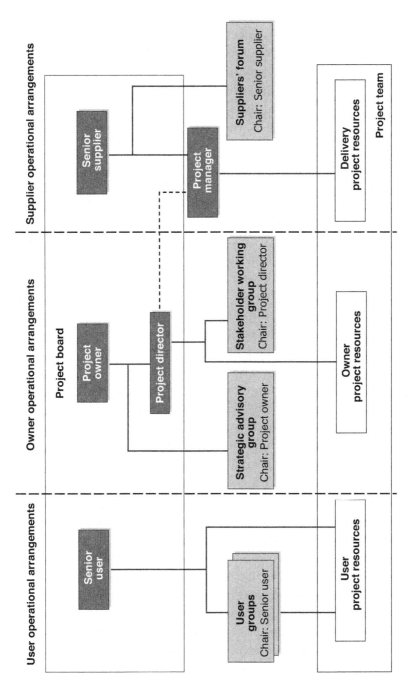

Figure 6.2 Project resourcing – the project board perspective

interests on a day-to-day basis. The project owner and project director are likely to need business resources assisting in the project definition and development. As the project progresses, these resources ensure the project continues to follow a path that will deliver the benefits required by the project owner and the business. The project owner chairs the stakeholder advisory group and uses this group to assist in defining the project and its course. Similarly, the project director works with the stakeholder working group (as well as the stakeholder advisory group), albeit at a more technical level.

Note that the project manager is shown as a part of the senior supplier's operational base. While this may not necessarily be the case, it is likely to be. It may be difficult for the senior supplier to ensure the quality of the end product if there is no contractual relationship between themselves and the project manager. Irrespective of the specific arrangement, it does not alter the fact that the key project decisions are made by the project board. If the project manager is an in-house appointment, it is likely that they report, in a line management sense, through to the senior supplier in the organization's chain of command, since both are likely to be employed within the project management arm of the organization (rather than the service delivery side of the organization). If the project manager is contracted in, their contract is likely to be with the project management side of the organization and the senior supplier may well be the 'contract manager'. Through the project manager, the senior supplier has the bulk of the project team resources at their disposal, although the management of those resources is, in the main, through the project manager. The exceptions are the business and user resources that work for the project owner/project director and senior user respectively. If there are multiple suppliers on the project, the senior supplier may wish to form a supplier's forum to ensure supplier issue management is addressed.

The senior user may wish to appoint user resources to the project. Full-time resources will not always be necessary. While it is likely that there will always be users associated with any project, the extent to which those users need to interact with the project is project specific. What is important is that there is a user presence throughout the project to ensure that on completion it meets users' needs and also to ensure ongoing user support for the project. Certain projects will benefit from the establishment of a user group, normally chaired by the senior user. Typically, these are ICT-enabled projects or business change projects, where a high degree of supported change is a prerequisite for success. For instance, if an organization were to establish a project for the implementation of this project governance framework, a user group is likely to be of benefit in achieving buy-in.

In a large organization that is constantly delivering projects, it is likely that project owners, senior suppliers, senior users and project directors will fulfil these roles on multiple projects. If not, it may create a resourcing problem within the organization as it struggles to identify different individuals for each project board role for each project. There are various means of structuring project governance arrangements to allow project owners and other project board role holders to have involvement in multiple projects whilst minimizing the resourcing burden on the organization.

Figure 6.3 shows various permutations for addressing the project governance needs of a group of projects. Diagram (a) shows one project owner acting in that role for a number of projects. In diagram (b), the project owner is supported by a project director on one of the projects, possibly one with more complexity or higher risk. Finally, in diagram (c), the project owner is supported by two project directors whilst still owning one project directly. In each instance, each project should still have a project board with the roles of senior supplier and senior user; those who fill those roles may do so on multiple projects.

Determining which projects require project directors and which projects the project owner 'owns' directly is dependent upon a number of factors. It may be related to the skill set required for the project, eg a particular project may require technical knowledge or skills different to those possessed by the project owner. Project owner time and availability constraints are likely to be factors, and the appointment of a project director will reduce the project owner's workload. Finally, one project may be so critical to the ongoing success of the organization that the project owner determines that their direct involvement is necessary.

This same approach can be applied when dealing with project boards – that is, to have a single project board running a number of projects. This approach is acceptable providing the members on the project board meet the membership requirements of each project. There is no point in having a senior user who has no user interest in one of the projects that falls under the governance of the overarching project board.

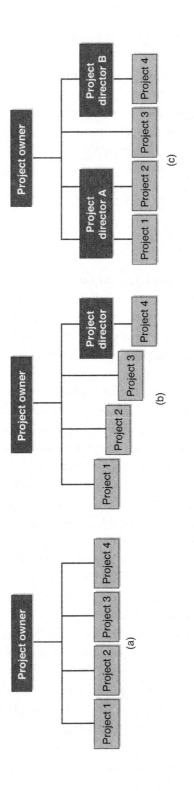

Figure 6.3 Options for project owners with project portfolios

In the event that the senior supplier is a representative of the in-house delivery arm of the organization, they may similarly wish to group projects for convenience, with a single senior supplier fulfilling that role for a number of projects. In-house delivery arms commonly operate in this manner.

Finally, it is not advisable to introduce the role of a senior project owner who oversees the activities of other project owners, because this begins to blur accountability. It is unclear then who takes responsibility for the success of the project in such circumstances and the split of responsibilities becomes confusing. Potentially, such a role also creates confusion with the role of programme owner, if such a role exists within the organization. Instead, it is better to consider appointing project directors to assist an overstretched project owner, or alternatively consider recruiting additional people who can fulfil project owner roles.

Executive summary: Implementing the framework

Implementing the change:

- establish the need;
- gain top management commitment to the need to change;
- gain broader support through:
  - user groups;
  - pilots;
  - trial periods.

Anticipate issues around:

- culture:
  - perceived loss of power by 'project management' groups;
  - delegation of authority and responsibility to project board;
- corporate policy gaps and conflicts;
- organizational issues where budget, service delivery and outcome are not aligned;
- resourcing and skills.

Case study 3: The challenges of implementation at the Department of Main Roads, Queensland Government

This case study covers the early phases of the implementation of this project governance framework in a major government roads department.

The drive for change in Queensland

Queensland is Australia's fastest growing state. In 2006/07 the economy expanded by 4.9 per cent, compared with national growth of 3.2 per cent. Over the past 10 years, gross state product has increased at an average rate of 4.8 per cent compared with the Australian average of 3.5 per cent. Economic growth and a sunny climate have resulted in significant population growth, particularly in the more populous south-east of the state, with approximately 1,000 people moving to the South East Queensland region each week. This growth has placed a strain on the region's infrastructure and the Queensland Government responded by releasing the SEQ Infrastructure Plan and Program (SEQIPP) in 2005 (Office of Urban Management, Queensland Government, 2007). This rolling 20-year plan outlines the projects and programmes that will deliver the new infrastructure. It details actual projects that are either planned or further advanced as well as studies that will eventually lead to projects. The latest annual release of SEQIPP includes $107 billion of identified projects. Transport infra-structure accounts for around 63 per cent of the total investment detailed in SEQIPP.

To assist in the delivery of this major programme of work, the Queensland Government established the Program Management Office (PMO) with the dual functions of 1) providing an oversight and reporting function of SEQIPP and 2) seeking opportunities to improve the efficiency and capacity of project delivery. The PMO resides within the Department of Infrastructure and Planning, a central government agency, and comprised a partnership between government and private sector advisors. While the PMO had influence, it had no control over the line agencies that were responsible for delivering their capital programmes. The PMO could advise but not instruct, and accountability for delivery remained with the line agencies that owned the projects.

One of the chief delivery concerns was the time it took projects, particularly large and complex projects, to reach construction. It was thought this may be due to inefficient decision-making processes and I was asked if I could assist the PMO in establishing more efficient project governance arrangements across government. This case study focuses on one Queensland Government agency in the initial stages of its implementation of the new project governance arrangements.

About the Department of Main Roads

Main Roads owns and manages the state-controlled road network in Queensland which, at 33,500 kilometres, is the longest of any state or territory in Australia. It is, for the most part, a high-speed road network connecting major centres across Queensland and interstate. It comprises long lengths of roads carrying traffic volumes ranging from less than 50 vehicles per day (vpd) to more than 140,000 vpd. The replacement value of the network is around $35 billion. Queensland's road network is the state government's largest publicly owned physical infrastructure asset and services the needs of over 4 million people (Queensland Department of Main Roads, 2007). Main Roads has a staff of around 4,000.

By 2005, Main Roads was facing a major increase in its capital programme as a result of Queensland's growth, and its projects featured prominently in SEQIPP. Its Roads Implementation Program (RIP) (capital and operating) had grown from around $5 billion in 2003/04 to $13.3 billion in 2007/08, an increase of 160 per cent in four years (see Figure 6.4). Whereas a few years previously headline projects were those above $100 million, that threshold had now grown to $1 billion.

There was recognition within Main Roads that if the increased works programme were to be delivered within budget and particularly time constraints, it would necessitate the department using more efficient

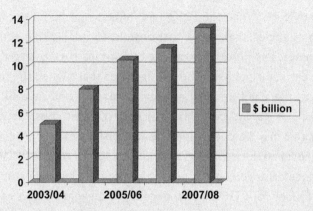

Figure 6.4   Growth in Main Roads RIP funding

project delivery mechanisms. It was within this environment that the PMO began discussions with various senior executives in Main Roads regarding improved project governance arrangements.

Project governance in Main Roads

Around 2002/03, senior executives in Main Roads recognized the organization had issues with its project delivery approach. Project costs were significantly exceeding budget even if contributing factors such as optimism bias were stripped out, and schedule overruns were becoming more prevalent. When these overruns occurred on large, highly visible projects, it reflected badly on the organization. These problems were in danger of creating an image within government that it was not receiving value for money from Main Roads and, given the competition for funding with other agencies in government, this could eventually have serious impacts for the organization.

To address this problem, Main Roads introduced a project delivery mechanism called OnQ along with a programme of project management training. OnQ provides a route map for project delivery. It details the steps a project should follow to take it through the planning phases and up to construction. It is a process map that ensures projects within the organization are delivered in a consistent manner. As a result of the introduction of OnQ project delivery has improved in Main Roads, although changing the culture of the organization is ongoing.

OnQ included a project governance module but there were many in the organization who felt it didn't fully meet their needs. Interestingly, this became most apparent not on Main Roads' projects, but on busways projects in which Main Roads were key stakeholders but not the project owner. Busways provide dedicated bus corridors that have lower whole-of-life costs than rail corridors and offer more flexible operating arrangements. Being public transport, they are funded by Queensland Transport, which acts as project owner. Upon completion of these projects, Main Roads becomes the owner of the corridor asset and is responsible for the maintenance of the asset. Main Roads therefore has a significant interest in the development of the project and yet was having problems engaging with the projects and was often not invited to project steering committee meetings. The OnQ project governance arrangements did not make it clear how key stakeholders could engage with the project; in fact it often left project owners wondering the same thing since it focused decision making in the asset delivery area rather than the service delivery area.

When the PMO proposed the new project governance arrangements to senior executives in the organization, they were able to identify immediate benefits that would flow from its implementation, given its emphasis on the role of the project owner and its structured engagement of stakeholders.

Change management approach in Main Roads

The PMO was a joint team comprised of government and private sector staff and the manner in which we operated was very much a partnership also. When we approached other government agencies it was always as a joint team – as advisor, I was always accompanied by a government officer. This helped avoid any perception that the change was being driven by forces external to government. Also, when the advisors transitioned out of the PMO, government officers were well placed for a seamless transition. Finally, it helped in ensuring the change was sustainable as opposed to a consultancy outcome that withers over time.

The senior executives within Main Roads who had most to gain from the new project governance arrangements were project owners. The new arrangements would provide them with greater control of their projects than under the previous OnQ governance arrangements. For the major projects, which were our initial focus, project owners were a relatively small group of district managers.

Buy-in to a new concept generally accompanies ownership of that concept. With new policy or change, ownership is an incremental process. It is very difficult to take a finished change product such as new project governance arrangements to an organization and expect them to embrace it. Instead, it helps if they play a part in shaping the product. We therefore approached these senior managers not with the finished version of the project governance arrangements but with a blank sheet of paper. In the initial meetings we sketched out the four principles of effective project governance and explained how the project governance model could be developed from them and the benefits the new arrangements would deliver. We then sought their opinions. Each of these experienced managers had already encountered the project delivery issues that the principles were designed to overcome and so, to an extent, we were preaching to the converted. Generally this will be the case where project governance is an issue in an organization, providing the initial discussions are held with service delivery managers. These are the executives with the most to gain from this project governance framework.

Meetings were followed up with a short paper that described the project governance arrangements. Many subsequent meetings were held with various executives to ensure that decision makers across the organization fully understood both the need for the revised arrangements and how they operated.

Mandating change

Mandating new policy or change is always an option. However, mandating does not necessarily imply the new policy or change will be used or be effective. If people don't support the new change, they may pay lip service to it while quietly ignoring it. Or they may not understand it and therefore use it ineffectively.

Mandating is not an alternative to change management; rather it is the last step in the change process. Only when people have accepted the new policy or change will they be open to its being mandated. They will then view mandating as a logical extension of the change process rather than the imposition of unwanted change.

Apart from role descriptions associated with the main project board roles, very little further documentation was provided. This enabled the organization to develop the concepts further to suit their own needs. Had the resources been available, it may have been preferable to offer ongoing support and training within the organization to assist in embedding the change. Ongoing support to Main Roads consisted primarily of assisting them to apply the new arrangements to new projects and ensuring that no misunderstandings had crept into the environment. For instance, the role of project director is always ripe for misunderstanding since this role invariably means different things to different organizations. Main Roads was no exception and we had to clarify and reinforce the definition of that role carefully. Further clarification was required in the relationship between the project manager and the project owner. If the project governance structure is treated as an organizational reporting arrangement – which it isn't – then it appears the project manager reports to the project owner. But as discussed earlier, the project governance structure is about decision making, not reporting. In large organizations it is more likely that the project manager has a line manager who is different to the project owner. In the case of Main Roads, a dedicated project delivery group – the Major Projects Office – has been established and project managers generally reported within this group. This created some confusion and in response we developed the structure shown in Figure 6.2, which shows the resources managed by each project board member.

The Main Roads perspective

I discussed the Main Roads perspective of the project governance framework and its implementation with Eddie Peters, who, as metropolitan district manager for Main Roads, is project owner for some of the largest road projects in Queensland, covering the greater Brisbane area.

Eddie commented that the new project governance arrangements provided new clarity and structure to the project decision-making framework in Main Roads. When Eddie and I first met there was already some concern that the role of the project owner was not being fully recognized in Main Roads and this was causing difficulties in ensuring optimum project outcomes. Thus the new arrangements, with their focus on the role and accountability of the project owner, were well received. Eddie commented early in our discussions in relation to the four principles that 'we already know most of this – it's just that it hasn't been packaged before'. This view is likely to be relevant to many readers. The principles in particular are individually intuitive – it is their integration and incorporation within a framework that provides the real benefit.

Eddie is very clear on the benefits that the new project governance framework has delivered. Foremost was the formal structure the new framework provides, where all executives involved in the project are clear on their particular responsibilities and how they relate to each other in the project space. In particular, Eddie raised the clarity and understanding the new framework brings to the role of the project owner along with that position's relationship with the senior supplier, senior user and the project director.

Eddie also commented favourably on the structure the new framework provides regarding the inclusion of stakeholders in the decision-making process. Whereas previously the approach to stakeholder involvement was ad hoc, the new arrangements formalized the approach.

I was also keen to understand any concerns Eddie had with the new project governance arrangements. The one concern he identified was an issue also mentioned above and related to clarity around the project director role. In the text it was mentioned that this term is often used within organizations to mean very different things. In Main Roads, project director was a role within the asset delivery arm of the business, Major Projects Office. The Major Projects Office is a specialist project management group. Their project director's role, which to avoid confusion we shall refer to as the asset delivery project director, encompassed overall project management delivery responsibility of a portfolio of projects each with its own project manager. Such an arrangement is perfectly valid from the perspective of the Major Projects Office. What is important is that all concerned recognize that this is not the context in which project director is being used in this text. Hence, in such circumstances, unless the project owner is intending to fulfil the project director's responsibilities themselves, they will still need to appoint their own project director.

The project governance arrangement is sufficiently flexible to address a role such as the asset delivery project director position, and a number of options are available. The option is dependent upon the special circumstances of each project:

- The asset delivery project director could fill the senior supplier role and the project manager report to the project board.
- The asset delivery project director could be considered as a role internal to the Major Projects Office and not play a role in the governance of that particular project.
- The asset delivery project director could report to the project board, effectively taking the project manager role for the project.

The confusion around the terminology in Main Roads illustrates the importance of ensuring all roles are clearly defined, and avoiding wherever possible conflicting terminology.

Eddie advised that, culturally, the new arrangements are proving something of a challenge, but no more than any other significant process change. There will always be early adopters and there will always be those that take a little longer to accept a new way of doing things. Eddie's view was firmly that if the process and systems are robust, as is the case with this project governance framework, and they are supported by training and ongoing health checks, then the necessary cultural change will be a matter of 'when', not 'if'. Main Roads had previously used dedicated trainers to drive cultural change in their project delivery areas but with mixed success. They have since moved towards a mentoring approach where experienced personnel make themselves available to project leaders on both a formal and informal basis, sharing their experience. This approach may be used to assist in the roll-out of the new project governance arrangements, although the mentors themselves will require training.

The resourcing issue has proven to be challenging for Main Roads. There is, as we discuss in the text, a need to build up the project owner's resources under this model so that the project owner can discharge their responsibilities effectively and fully. The issue faced within Main Roads is similar to that faced by many organizations that deliver large projects on a regular basis. The asset delivery arm of the organization has been relatively well resourced, but the customer or service delivery side of the organization has not received the same recognition in terms of the resources required in the project space. This imposes considerable resource constraints on project owners. It remains an ongoing issue.

Finally I asked Eddie about the approach we, in the Program Management Office, took to implementing the change across Main Roads. He considered our 'softly-softly' approach, to be much preferable to a mandating approach, which as a central agency we perhaps could have used – refer to the text box above. Eddie did have a criticism of our approach in that the perception he gained was that we automatically assumed the existing Main Roads OnQ methodology needed to change without first exploring with Main Roads that this need existed. This is, of course, is a fundamental failing in any business change undertaking. While I had studied the OnQ methodology's project governance arrangements and considered them somewhat lacking, no effort had been made to express our concerns to Main Roads executives. The first step in any change process is establishing the need and doing so with those that will have to change; an important step in gaining credibility with the organization. This step involves mapping out the current state and identifying what issues exist in respect of that process. Only then should thoughts turn to identifying how the situation could be improved through process change. It was the problem identification step that was missed here. We perhaps got away with it on this occasion because the people we were dealing with in Main Roads were relatively open to change and had already identified a need to do so.

7 The governance relationship between programmes and projects

The programme

Every project should be aligned with corporate goals. Without this alignment, the outcomes the project delivers may not further those goals. Therefore each project seeks to be consistent with the overall vision and strategy of the organization. However, the link between the project's objectives and the organization's vision and strategy are not always obvious at the project level since the project is separated from the high-level corporate strategy by many layers of detail and scope. Also, it is quite likely that a combination of projects are required to produce the benefits that clearly support the organization's goals. Individual projects will contribute to the overall realization of benefits but, in themselves, may not produce the outcome required by the organization. For example: an upgraded motorway may only shift traffic congestion from one point to another, whereas an upgraded road network achieves the benefit of reduced travel times; a new local hospital may reduce waiting times for patients, but as part of a new regional health plan can deliver the benefit of fewer patients needing to go to hospital; a new port facility might increase the capacity of the port but highlight constraints in the supporting rail network – on the other hand, the port upgrade as part of an integrated freight network delivers the benefit of greater freight throughput.

Thus is born the concept of the programme. A programme is an interconnected group of projects, managed as an entity so that they deliver benefits. In theory, each project delivers outputs, whereas the overall programme delivers outcomes that enable benefits to be realized. So in the port example above, individual projects might include the upgrade of the port and the upgrade of the rail link (the outputs), the overall programme delivers increased freight throughput (the outcome) and this delivers benefits such as increased profitability to port users and the port owner, and increased tax revenue for the government. The outcomes and benefits are delivered either over the course of the programme or upon its completion. As the various projects are delivered, so certain benefits are realized, although it may take combinations of projects to deliver particular benefits. Because the programme has a strong focus on strategic benefits, it provides the critical linkage between the project and the organization. In doing so, it should establish the framework within which the project is to deliver. Much is being made lately of programme management, possibly because it is now apparent that it is insufficient in itself to successfully deliver a project; it's just as important to deliver the right project at the right time. This is the role of the programme.

The linkages between the projects within a programme vary from being tightly interwoven to relatively loose. The 1998 Programme case study on the introduction of full retail contestability to the England and Wales electricity market (see case study 2 at the end of Chapter 4) is an example of a programme of tightly interrelated projects. In that case study, each project was so interlinked with its neighbours that failure of any one project would have seriously impacted the realization of any benefits from the programme.

Even projects that may appear to be quite different can be closely interrelated from a programme perspective and require a programme approach to ensure the realization of benefits. For example, the construction, fit-out and staffing of a new tertiary hospital to meet the needs of a growing community could be considered a single, stand-alone project. However, the community will not realize the full benefits of the new hospital without adequate transport links and so the delivery of the hospital needs to be coordinated, say, with an upgraded road network in the area and a new rail station. There may therefore be three major projects that require coordination and management to ensure the full benefit of 'increased health care' is realized. These projects may therefore form the constituent projects of a larger programme. (The delivery of the hospital itself could be structured as a programme since there are very specific interrelated components within the delivery including building construction, facilities management, specialist equipment, staffing, etc.).

In large programmes containing many projects, not all projects are necessarily interrelated. The Queensland Government released the South East Queensland Infrastructure Plan and Programme (SEQIPP), which currently (2008) details an approximate investment of $107 billion in infrastructure development across the region and contains about 300 projects. Many projects that are geographically close within SEQIPP have strong interrelationships, similar to those of the hospital example quoted above. On the other hand, projects in the north of the region have little relationship to those in the south, given their geographical remoteness from each other. However, all are linked through the common vision of the programme, 'to deliver a sustainable future for South East Queensland'.

In most organizations, projects are part of a wider programme of work. It would be unusual to identify a project that was not linked sufficiently closely to other projects to warrant being part of a programme of work that encompassed other projects. The projects that comprise a programme may be of any type – they may be policy projects, business change, infrastructure, ICT, etc.

The programme owner

Like projects, programmes require clear ownership. Because a programme may involve many projects, and potentially projects in different sectors, identifying the owner of a programme is not always as clear cut as it is for projects (refer to the text box on cross-sector programmes, page 138). When the projects comprising a programme all reside within the same area of the organization it makes sense that the programme owner is a senior officer within that part of the organization.

Cross-sector programmes

It can be difficult to establish cross-sector programmes. Take as an example the development of a new tertiary hospital that was discussed above. The programme in this case could involve the hospital itself and its various sub-projects, a major road upgrade and a major public transport upgrade. Each of the three main projects derives from different sectors.

Identifying a programme owner for this programme will be difficult. The approach for identifying project owners involved identifying the person who matched the main characteristics of the role: having responsibility for service delivery, since ownership of the service to be delivered conferred ownership of the project that would enable the service; and owning the funding of the project since budget accountability implied project accountability. In this example, neither of these pointers will provide a simple answer. The services to be delivered by a hospital are very different to those being delivered by public transport and roads. Therefore ownership will be very different. Similarly the budgets will be divided by government agency.

There are three possible options for delivering such a programme:

1. Select the programme owner from the largest and most complex of the projects comprising the programme, even though they are unlikely to have the necessary understanding of each sector.
2. Programme ownership could be vested with a person of sufficient authority in a central agency or head office division who therefore has oversight of all constituent projects, even though they may have little knowledge of the sectors from which some of those project derive.
3. Alternatively, the organization relies on the governance and stakeholder management of individual projects to ensure a coordinated outcome across all associated projects. This approach doesn't treat the constituent projects as a true programme but rather recognizes the strong interdependencies between projects and manages them at the individual project level.

Government generally uses approach 3) since each project in an example like this is normally part of its own programme with funding, programme ownership and management in place. This approach requires careful coordination of project activities between agencies. While this is difficult, it has already been shown how a project can achieve this through judicious stakeholder management. In this example, while each project has its strategic advisors' group, it would probably be advisable to introduce coordinating committees at both the project owner level and officer level.

The programme owner provides leadership for the programme and must therefore have the necessary authority. This implies they hold a senior position within the organization. As part of that leadership function, the programme owner is accountable for the success of the programme – just as the project owner is accountable for the success of a project. There is no conflict between these two accountabilities. Simplistically, if a single project within the programme fails, then questions are asked of the project owner. If a large number of projects within the programme fail, then questions must be asked of the programme owner since there is the implication of systemic failure in the programme delivery arrangements. The programme owner ensures that the programme is designed to meet the strategy and vision of the organization and that this alignment between the organization's goals and the programme's objectives continues throughout the life of the programme.

The programme owner ensures the programme is adequately funded. This will require detailed funding plans for the first few years plus higher-level estimates for later years. The funding plans should also incorporate estimates of recurrent costs (debt servicing, operations and maintenance costs) to ensure the organization is prepared to meet future commitments resulting from the delivered projects.

The programme owner establishes the programme governance arrangements and the programme office. They are supported in their activities by peers normally drawn from divisions or agencies whose projects comprise the programme as well as central agency or 'whole of corporation' business units or divisions – perhaps a representative of the CEO's office. These representatives form the programme board or programme sponsoring group or programme steering committee – the terminology is relatively unimportant, although the OGC publication *Managing Successful Programmes* (OGC, 2007) differentiates between the programme sponsoring group and the programme board, thereby separating the sponsoring or championing activity from the control and decision-making activity, which may be a useful approach in large organizations. What is important is that the group represents the interests of the organization and ensures that the programme continues at all times to deliver outcomes that will support the organization's vision and goals.

Decision making at the programme level

The fourth principle of effective project governance is separation of project governance from corporate or organizational governance. This avoids constraining the project with hierarchical decision-making chains that can slow its decision-making processes. The presence of an overarching programme within which the project sits provides even greater confidence that the project decision-making arrangements can be removed from that of the organization structure. This is because it is at the programme level that delivery of projects becomes entwined with the decision making of the organization. The role of the programme board is to ensure the direction of the programme matches and supports the direction of the organization. Since the programme exists to enable and further the strategy of the organization, strategic decision making at the programme level and strategic decision making at the corporate level are tightly linked.

The programme board is responsible for ensuring the programme is aligned with the organization's strategy and throughout its life continues to meet the objectives of the organization. It should oversee periodic reviews of the programme designed to ensure that, among others things, the programme remains both on track and aligned to the organization's strategy. Members of the programme board champion the programme within their respective areas and should represent the visible face of the programme to the organization.

The day-to-day running of the programme is undertaken by the programme office. However, there will be issues, including some elevated by projects within the programme, that are beyond the remit of the programme office to resolve and the programme board will be expected to address such issues. At a programme level, some such issues are likely to impact on the policy and strategy of the organization. For example, large programmes could encounter issues associated with:

● Funding: there may be problems funding the entire programme or the funding envelope may vary over time according to the revenue streams of the organization. When this happens it may be necessary for the programme board to take decisions regarding re-sequencing of the programme, seeking new sources of funding or even dropping projects from the programme.

- Resourcing: a large programme of work can have an impact on the availability of resources within the organization. In the government environment, large programmes can also have an impact on the general availability of resources in the market as a whole.
- Supplier and materials availability: not normally a problem for the private sector but, again, large government programmes can place a strain on the market, which will take some time to respond.
- Price escalation: high demand driven by large programmes of work will drive up prices and this may start to have an impact on the affordability envelope of the programme.

The programme board approves key programme documentation, which is likely to include the following:

- The programme business case provides the justification for the programme through an assessment of the benefits of delivering the programme against the costs and risks of doing so. At this early stage, while there may be little detail, some level of cost estimation will be necessary from both a future funding perspective and to more accurately assess the overall justification for the programme. It is likely that past projects can provide some indication of both capital and recurrent costs associated with the project.
- The benefits plan identifies the benefits expected to be delivered by the programme, the timing of the delivery of those benefits, the means by which benefits will be measured, the linkage between benefits and the projects within the programme, etc.
- The programme plan identifies the projects that comprise the plan, their approximate schedules and anticipated cost/cash flow information, risk assessment of the programme, etc. The plan should also address the interfaces and dependencies between the various projects that comprise the programme.

The parameters that define the development of individual projects must be included in the documentation – where they sit is less important than the fact that they exist. Some of this information is already covered within the documents described above, such as the anticipated cost of the projects and their delivery schedules. The quality parameters for the programme should be established in as much detail as is necessary to provide individual projects with clear direction regarding the necessary quality criteria. For instance, in a transport programme, the level of quality of rolling stock should be defined and be consistent as far as possible across the programme. This avoids individual projects setting de facto standards that subsequently have an impact on other projects in the programme and provides guidance to projects where no equivalent or comparative projects exist. Without this information, projects are forced to operate in a strategic and/or policy vacuum and to develop their own parameters. This risks the overall programme lacking consistency and having a blurred vision of the outcomes being sought.

The role of the programme office

The programme office supports the programme board in managing the programme. The office is led by a programme manager who reports to the programme owner. The role of the programme office includes the following activities, although in some cases the manner in which these activities are treated may be laid down by corporate head office or a central agency to ensure consistency across the entire organization rather than establish different approaches in different programmes:

- establishing reporting requirements for the programme. This includes programme reporting as well as defining the reporting requirements of individual projects – how often they report and what they are to report upon. Standard templates are normally developed;
- establishing the financial parameters that trigger exception reports. The programme owner requires notification if a project is heading towards significant over- or under-spend. First, though, the programme office must define what constitutes 'significant' and this may be different for different projects. A 10 per cent overrun on a $50 million project will have a different impact to a 10 per cent overrun on a $500 million project in the same programme;
- defining scheduling parameters that trigger exception reports. As for financial parameters, notification is required if there is a likelihood that a project within the programme could fail to meet its agreed deadlines. Again, there may be different trigger points for different projects,

depending on whether a project's delivery, or one of its deliverables, is a prerequisite for another project. Alternatively, the success criteria for a particular project may require project completion at a specific time;

- defining KPIs linked to planned benefits so that the organization can measure the effectiveness of programme outcomes;
- establishing the configuration management approach that the programme will adopt, including change control and version control;
- defining the project development methodology. While this should be established as policy across the organization, in the event that it is not, the programme office should establish some basic requirements to which constituent project developments must adhere. As a minimum, this will include establishing the documentation expected of each project (such as preliminary business case, project plan, final business case and so on);
- developing and managing programme risk. Each project in the programme will, or should, have its own risk register and risk management plan. There may be certain project level risks that can have an impact on the programme. For instance, failure to deliver a key project in time in an event-driven programme may place at risk the entire programme. The programme office should have a good understanding of potential project risks that could have an impact on the programme. There may also be risks that the entire programme faces, such as the potential for cost escalation, resource shortages, funding issues, industrial relations issues, statutory changes and so on. Some projects within the programme will be commissioned before others, in which case there may be operational risks associated with those projects. For instance, industrial relations issues arising at a newly commissioned facility may spill over onto other projects;
- scheduling and sequencing of projects within the programme. The programme office should advise on the optimum sequencing and scheduling of projects to better manage the constraints upon the programme, for example affordability and resource constraints. By changing the sequencing of projects, it may be possible to ease these constraints without unduly compromising the realization of benefits and their timing;
- offering project support through centre of excellence activities. In a programme of work that crosses sectors, agencies or organizational divisions, it may be that some areas of the organization are less proficient than others in delivering projects. The programme

office may offer services to these areas to support their project delivery activities. This may include, for example, business case development support (remembering that irrespective of any support offered, the Business Case is still owned by the project owner), facilitation of risk workshops, etc.

The relationship between programme and project governance

A comparison between the roles of project owner and programme owner indicates a number of parallels. The project owner is accountable for the success of the project and has budget accountability. The project owner holds a service delivery role in the organization; the successful delivery of the project will enable them to continue to deliver that service at the required level.

The programme owner is accountable for the success of the programme and as such holds a senior position within the organization. The programme owner holds budget accountability for the programme. The programme owner may have a service delivery role in the organization that is dependent upon the successful outcome of the programme, but this will not always be the case. The programme owner and programme board may identify and appoint project owners, although again, depending on the structure of the programme, this may not be appropriate. The programme office may assist the organization by providing guidelines around the selection of project owners.

The programme owner may sit within the project's strategic advisors' group, depending upon the importance of the project to the overall programme. If the project is central to the success of the programme, it may be that the programme owner also takes on the role of project owner for that project. This should only occur where the programme owner's position in the organization justifies taking on that role in line with the earlier discussions in Chapters 3 and 4. Note that for the programme owner to assume the project owner role implies the project is of such importance that the programme itself would be compromised if that project were to 'fail' – ie run significantly over budget, behind schedule or its output not meet the service delivery need. The programme owner may assume a position on the project board other than project owner; however, this should again only occur on a project that is central to the success of the programme; it should not happen as a matter of course, since the programme owner is not necessarily best placed to fill project board roles.

The project owner and project board are concerned with risks and issues that have an impact on the project. The programme owner and programme board are concerned with risks and issues that can have an impact on the programme as a whole, albeit that some of these may be escalated from individual projects.

The programme owner is responsible for securing funding for the programme. A programme is allocated a budget and a project will be allocated a budget within the programme. A programme budget does not absolve an individual project from development of a business case to justify the organization's commitment to it. The effort that goes into any business case will depend on the project's risk profile within the programme. Similarly, not all investment decisions will need to be approved by the investment decision group; lower-risk projects could be approved at the programme level or even the project board level, depending on the delegations that have been established. The programme owner is accountable for the programme budget as defined within the programme business case. The project owners are accountable for project budgets as defined in project business cases. The programme owner is responsible for setting and adjusting project priorities, scheduling and scope to ensure the programme remains within its budget. The programme office maintains an overview of the programme's cash flow implications and reports this to the organization's treasury. This activity should also take into consideration the recurrent cost implications of the programme, including debt servicing costs, maintenance and operational costs. This information will feed into treasury calculations regarding the envelope of affordability for this and other programmes. This envelope will have a number of constraints, including the debt level beyond which the organization's credit rating is compromised and the level of recurrent expenditure compared with revenue, particularly if the organization is averse to borrowing to fund recurrent expenditure.

A programme must ensure ongoing alignment with the vision and objectives of the organization, which potentially could change over the duration of a long programme. The outcomes and benefits that programmes deliver must therefore continue to support the core objectives of the organization should these change. Projects should not need to justify their existence in terms of their alignment with the organization's vision, goals or objectives – that is the role of the programme – and providing the project is developed within the parameters set down by the programme, this alignment should already have been established. The programme therefore establishes the strategic link between the project and the organization. Projects cannot develop within a vacuum. They need parameters that guide their development and it is the programme documentation that provides these parameters.

The programme owner and programme board approve the key programme documentation, while the project board approves key project documentation. The project owner is responsible for ensuring the project remains within the parameters set by the programme and provides reports and updates to the programme office. An effective relationship between the programme and its constituent projects requires a partnering approach. A poor relationship establishes the programme office as little more than a reporting house and even then the quality of the reported information is probably suspect – more what the project wants the programme office and senior management to see rather than what they need to see.

Executive summary: Project owner versus programme owner

Project owner	Programme owner
Accountable for project success	Accountable for programme success
Holds project budget accountability	Holds programme budget accountability
Holds service delivery role	May hold service delivery role May appoint project owners
Approves key project documentation	Approves key programme documentation
Addresses project risks	Addresses programme risks
Ensures project aligned to programme	Ensures programme aligned to corporate goals
Chairs project board	May chair project board of programme-critical project May sit on strategic advisors' group

8 Towards an integrated project delivery framework

In conducting their operational activities, organizations strive towards efficient business processes, knowing that the more efficient the process the lower the cost to the organization. The same concept holds for the delivery of the organization's capital programme and is one of the drivers for the adoption of project management methodologies. A project management methodology provides an organization with a consistent approach to the delivery of projects that ensures project officers and senior executives have a clear and common understanding of what to expect from any project at any time in its development. Thus a consistent project delivery approach within an organization makes their job easier and makes them more efficient and effective in undertaking their roles. This then increases the efficiency of the organization's delivery of its capital programme.

Of course all projects are different, so there is a limit to the degree of consistency that can be applied to project delivery, particularly across different industry sectors. However, while projects themselves are different, the development process through which they evolve has similarities. The closer projects resemble one another, the more similarities there are in their development processes. Yet, even dissimilar projects follow, or should follow, a high-level route map that guides them from their inception to project closure. Nobody disputes that ICT projects are very different from construction projects; however, there are certain elements that are or should be common to projects from all sectors. The elements of a project delivery framework include:

- project governance, where, as this text has shown, a common framework can be applied to projects from any sector;
- the key project documentation that supports project decision making;
- the major milestones that the project achieves over its life;
- the key approvals that the project must obtain over its life, including funding approvals;
- estimates of the project's likely cost over its development and the associated level of accuracy;
- major project assurance processes including stage gates.

These elements do not exist in isolation but are interrelated. The nature of these relationships develops over the course of the project – documentation changes, milestones are achieved, cost estimates firm, etc. If structured properly, these elements and the relationships between them can be developed into an integrated framework for project delivery. Because such an integrated project delivery framework is necessarily high level in order to ensure relevance across all industry sectors, it has the capacity to act as a valuable tool for senior executives. The organization that develops such a framework stands to benefit in a number of ways:

- The elements that comprise an integrated project delivery framework represent those aspects of the project with which senior executives are most engaged. These are the aspects that will be discussed in project board, investment decision group and strategic advisors' group meetings. The greater the level of consistency that an organization can develop in these areas, the greater the benefit to these executives. Decision makers will then address consistent key documentation, governance arrangements, key decisions, etc. irrespective of the type of project, or the sector or division within which it sits. From the senior executive perspective it represents a single framework for the delivery of all projects within the organization. For any executive sitting on the investment decision group or who regularly sits on project boards, it provides commonality of approach irrespective of the type of project being considered. Thus projects involving ICT, business change, infrastructure delivery or even policy will follow the same high-level route map to completion. All executives associated with projects in the organization know, at the strategic level, what is expected at any point throughout any project's lifecycle.

- With the consistency that a project delivery framework provides comes greater familiarity as project officers and senior executives continue to use the same approach on project after project. This enables more efficient resource utilization since less time is spent determining the process to be followed. It provides a baseline process for project delivery that enables the organization to state with confidence 'This is the way we deliver projects'.
- Project officers on all projects are aware what is required of them in respect of project delivery. This facilitates movement of project officers across the organization since learning curves will be reduced in duration.
- The investment decision group regularly makes investment decisions on very different projects from different sectors. This group will therefore benefit from a clear and consistent approach followed by all projects.
- The quality of key project documentation will increase since best practice and learnings can be readily shared across the organization.
- There may also be less tangible benefits from the adoption of an integrated project delivery framework. The market's appreciation of the organization will improve since the organization will present itself as having a clear approach to project delivery. The market will take confidence in its dealings with such an organization. The organization may also establish a better perception amongst its auditors, who will derive comfort through evidence of the consistent application of good process.
- Because the approach is high level, it does not stifle creativity and allows flexibility of delivery at the project level. An integrated project delivery framework need not be beholden to any particular project management methodology but can provide an overarching framework for delivery with which most recognized methodologies will be consistent.

In order to construct an integrated project delivery framework, it is necessary to have an understanding of the project lifecycle – the development process through which a project proceeds from its inception to its closure and operational state. This is important since the elements of a project delivery framework are integrated within the project lifecycle and are defined at key points in that lifecycle.

The phases of the project lifecycle

There are many examples of project lifecycles and they are all aiming to describe basically the same thing – how a project develops from its inception through to its closure. It can be as simple as 'plan–do–review' or it can be significantly more complex and sophisticated. The project lifecycle described below and in Figure 8.1 is therefore just one example; it's a little more complex than some since it has six stages, but each stage is supported by the elements of the project delivery framework mentioned above and therefore enables a one-to-one mapping between these elements.

Strategic assessment

The initial phase of a project involves establishing the business need for that project and addresses its strategic alignment with the organization. Projects should derive from a programme of work and the programme itself will have a strategic direction with benefits accruing from the combination of various constituent projects. The objectives of the project should align with that strategy and support the delivery of the overall programme benefits. This phase seeks to display a strong link between the desired outcomes of the project and those of the organization or programme. Strategic assessment spans programme and project activities. While all the activities detailed here should be conducted prior to the project proceeding to subsequent phases, some will be undertaken as programme activities, while others will be done within the remit of the project.

For instance, the ownership of the project is established as part of the strategic assessment and this activity is normally considered part of the programmes remit and, as discussed earlier, is the event that initiates the project. The project governance arrangements will provide the terms of reference of the various committees and the roles and responsibilities of those involved. Key stakeholders are also identified during

Figure 8.1 Typical project lifecycle

this period. The governance arrangements will need to be flexible since new stakeholders may be identified during the course of the project or may only become involved in the project further into its development – the change of senior supplier from advisor to contractor as the project progresses from development to build is a case in point.

The service delivery requirement or business need answers the question 'Why do we need this project?' The project is analysed to establish a clear link to corporate goals, normally through its contribution to the benefits of the overarching programme of which it is a part. A programme of projects will, as a package, deliver a range of benefits greater than the sum of the individual benefits of each project. Projects that are not strategically aligned with the programme may lose priority to avoid jeopardizing funding for projects essential to the realization of programme benefits.

There are a number of other activities that can be commenced during the strategic assessment but not completed until subsequent phases of the lifecycle. These include the following:

- selection for further analysis of a range of options for meeting the service delivery need, including non-asset solutions;
- initial risk workshops to identify and assess strategic risks;
- development of an initial project plan. Estimates of the delivery schedule will be based at this early stage on similar or analogous projects. If the project is part of a programme, there should already be a view as to when the project will be commenced and completed. Projects are often reluctant to establish a project plan at such an early stage, concerned that it may set expectations that cannot be subsequently revised. However, without an end date, there is no urgency to deliver and it is during the early project phases that the greatest delivery inefficiencies can occur;
- development of the first draft of the project's business case, referred to as the strategic business case. The business case is perhaps the single most important document to be developed over the course of the project. Its purpose is to provide the justification for undertaking the project, with reference to its strategic fit with the organization's goals and the programme of work of which it is (or may be) a component, the costs of its implementation, the risks it entails, and the benefits it will deliver. The strategic business case is used as a key input to the decision to proceed with the project.

Note that the business case is a live document that grows in both scope and detail over the course of the project. At this early stage the strategic business case will contain significant detail around business drivers, project objectives and stakeholders, while areas such as likely cost, delivery schedule and procurement options will be very high level. The initial indicative cost estimate is likely to be based upon comparisons with similar projects.

Strategic assessment: Summary of key decisions and key documentation

Key decision: whether to proceed with the project.

Decision makers will be asking:

- Is the project a strategic fit for the organization?
- Is there a strong business need?
- Is there support for the project from the key stakeholders?
- Do the benefits justify the costs and risks?

Key decision-making document: strategic business case.
    Other generic documentation may include: 1) outline project plan; 2) risk register.

Preliminary assessment

During the preliminary assessment phase the options identified in the strategic assessment are analysed in more detail and a shortlist of two or three is derived. The primary outcome of the preliminary assessment phase is the decision on whether to proceed with the development of a full business case that will compare these options and select a preferred option. Central to this decision are issues of affordability, risk and the priority of the project in relation to other demands for that funding from elsewhere in the organization. The inputs to this analysis include but are not limited to the following:

- Cost and affordability: the estimated cost of each option is a significant factor in its preferred ranking against other options. The cost equation has two components. The capital cost of the option will determine the extent of any borrowing required and the consequent impact upon debt levels, credit ratings and so forth. Each option will also have an associated recurrent cost comprised of debt servicing, operational and maintenance costs. Cost estimates at this stage of a project are normally based upon concept designs. The accuracy being sought for these estimates may be ± 50 per cent or better.

- Benefits: initial estimates are made of the benefits accruing from each option, enabling a benefit–cost ratio to be calculated for each.
- Options-based risk analyses: each option is assessed for risks, and the optimum allocation of risk between counterparties is considered. This allocation feeds into estimates of the cost (or benefit) associated with that risk, which are built into the option's estimates and cost–benefit calculations.
- Preliminary procurement strategy: consideration is given to the manner in which the project will be delivered and the contractual arrangements that will underpin the delivery. It is possible that different options may benefit from different procurement models. Factors influencing the choice of procurement model include the maturity of the technology, the maturity of the market and the organization in delivery of this type of project, its complexity, the risks associated with the project and the state of the market itself. Note that the risk analysis discussed above must also take into account the identified procurement model since the choice of model impacts the risks, their allocation and mitigation.
- Shortlist of options and ongoing development of the business case and project plan: the combination of the above activities culminates in a shortlist of options, normally two or three. A summary of the options analysis is usually incorporated within the business case, which has expanded from the original strategic business case into what is now a preliminary business case. It is this document that provides the primary input to the decision as to whether to develop a full business case. The analysis conducted on the various options and in particular that on the subsequently favoured options will include further assessment of the time frame for delivery, allowing the project plan to be refined.

Preliminary assessment: Summary of key decisions and key documentation

Key decision: whether to proceed with the development of a full business case.

Decision makers will be asking:

- Have all reasonable options been explored?
- Do the benefits justify the estimated costs and the risks?
- Are there other calls on the organization's resources that have a higher priority?

Key decision-making document: preliminary business case.
   Other generic documentation may include:

- risk register;
- options analysis;
- feasibility studies;
- preliminary procurement strategy;
- preliminary project plans for shortlisted options.

Business case development (including procurement strategy)

This phase of the lifecycle is sometimes split into the separate phases of business case development and procurement strategy. However, the business case cannot be developed in isolation of the procurement strategy since the chosen procurement model is likely to have an impact on basic parameters of the business case such as risk allocation and schedule. Different procurement models encourage different risk allocations and this in turn has an impact on the costing of the individual options. For this reason the two activities occur broadly concurrently.

The primary objectives of the business case development phase are to select the preferred project option, including the preferred delivery option, and to provide the justification for procuring this option. The final business case is used by senior management as the key document in deciding whether to proceed with the project by offering it to the market. The main activities during this phase are:

- Refining the project governance arrangements: if this is necessary to reflect the needs of the project as it is currently defined, it should be undertaken at the commencement of this phase. Note that changing an existing project governance structure may meet with resistance, so it is best when governance arrangements are established early in the project, as they should be, that these arrangements stand the test of time. So while this new stage in the project is an opportunity to revisit the project governance arrangements, it is advisable to do so with caution and some restraint.

- Conduct financial analysis: the financial analysis of options investigates the cost of the project to the organization and details both capital costs, including project development costs, and the whole-of-life costs of each option. The implications of a focus on capital cost alone have been discussed previously.

- Conduct a detailed risk analysis: the financial analysis will also be influenced by the risks facing the project. Taking a simple '15 per cent contingency' approach to valuing risk is not appropriate when dealing with large and complex projects. Individual risks should be quantified and, where possible, the cost of mitigation incorporated within the estimated project cash flow. Alternatively, a probabilistic approach to risk pricing may be warranted.

Key project documentation

It's easy to get confused when discussing the documentation that a project develops through its lifecycle. One organization's project brief is another's strategic business case, one methodology's project plan is another's implementation plan, and so on. However, all organizations should have a set of internally consistent key project documents that all projects must develop. Apart from supporting decision making, this avoids duplication of information across documents and avoids documents such as the business case being the repository for all sorts of information not necessarily associated with that document. The task is slightly complicated by overlaps between documents. For instance, the business case often contains summarized information from the project plan and the options analysis.

An organization that is starting from the position of effectively having nothing in place or, alternatively, has a quite muddled position,

> requires a starting point. PRINCE2 (OGC, 2005a) can provide that starting point. It is not necessary to fully implement PRINCE2, but its range of documentation is comprehensive and internally consistent. Choose what is necessary and leave the rest.

- Identify the procurement model: inherent within the development of the procurement strategy is the optimum allocation of risk between the project proponents. Different procurement models are designed to meet the specific needs of projects and organizations and allocate risks accordingly. A model that may be suitable for an organization for one project may be unsuitable for another. Conversely, it may be appropriate for different organizations to procure very similar projects using very different procurement models. It depends upon the project's risks and which party is best able to manage those risks – the client organization or the supplier. Each procurement model can be fine-tuned to ensure the optimum outcome.
- Conduct economic analysis: the economic analysis balances the benefits of undertaking the project against the costs and risks of doing so. Project benefits should be quantified wherever possible, including those attributable to the project that accrue from broad social, environmental and economic impacts. So, for instance, the benefits to an organization of meeting or exceeding environmental legislation may be more than just avoidance of fines, and could include a public relations benefit that flows through to revenue.

The project makes a recommendation on what it considers the preferred option both in terms of the project design and the method of procurement. The preferred option should be developed to a level of detail that enables the investment decision makers within the organization to have confidence that what is described, in terms of scope, cost, quality and schedule, accurately reflects what the project will deliver. This requires the development of a detailed cost plan, a detailed project plan through to completion of the project and information on the preferred procurement model. This information should reflect feedback obtained through engagement with the market.

Business case development: Summary of key decisions and key documentation

Key decision: there are two related decisions made at the end of the business case development stage. The first is whether the organization wishes to accept the recommendation of the business case and take the project to the market. Note that this assumes the business case recommends the project should proceed, which is normally the case since by this stage in the process the project team is very committed to the project and highly unlikely to recommend aborting it. For this reason the business case should always be robustly challenged on its recommendation.

The second decision is the means of procurement, which will also have been recommended by the project team. Note that if the organization accepts the decision to take the project to the market but challenges the model of procurement, this may necessitate the business case being revisited since the procurement model is an integral part of the business case. This is unlikely to happen in practice since the senior project team members will have kept decision makers appraised of project developments, ensuring substantive buy-in to the main recommendations, of which the procurement strategy will have been one.

Decision makers will be asking:

- Has the best value for money option for undertaking the project been selected?
- Do the benefits of undertaking this project outweigh the costs and risks associated with its development?
- Will the market respond positively and efficiently to the project?

Key decision-making documents: final business case and procurement strategy.
Other generic documentation may include:

- project plans for investigated options;
- specification/design for preferred option and preliminary designs for non-preferred options;
- detailed risk register.

Procurement

Traditionally, the procurement stage develops a shortlist of organizations that have the capability to undertake the work and then selects the preferred proponent based upon a bidding process involving the shortlisted organizations. The actual process is dependent upon the nature of the procurement model. The following description of a traditional procurement is sufficient for our needs. The nature of the procurement process is also influenced by the policies and culture of the organization. For instance, organizations with an in-house workforce may have policies that determine the extent to which the market is engaged on particular projects.

The development of a shortlist is achieved through an expression of interest (EOI) process where the market is informed of the nature of the project, its objectives, the outcomes the project is intended to deliver and the time frames in which the project is expected to deliver. The EOI process aims to identify those market participants capable of delivering the project. During the EOI process, the organization receives feedback from the market regarding the attractiveness of the project and the market's view of the major project risks and which party (contractor or client) is best placed to manage those risks. The output of the EOI process is usually a shortlist of around three potential bidders.

Once the shortlist is determined, the organization develops bid documentation to support the tendering process including:

- specification of the work, including design documentation;
- information regarding regulatory, environmental, heritage and other legal requirements;
- initial expectations regarding the allocation of risk between the parties;
- draft contract documentation;
- criteria for evaluation of bids and the bidding rules.

Tenders are then called and bids received and evaluated according to the evaluation criteria. The bids are also measured against the business case to ensure the market response fits within the technical, quality, cost and scheduling envelope described within it. If the bids fall outside these parameters, it will be necessary to revisit the business case to determine if the market response provides value for money. If it does not then the organization does not proceed with the project. Abandoning a large project at this stage has significant implications in respect of sunk costs of both the organization and tenderers, and also has an impact on the market's perception of the organization.

A bid evaluation report identifies the preferred tenderer and is used as the basis of the investment decision by the organization. If the organization has already approved the project's business case, then the investment decision has largely been made, providing the market response of the preferred tenderer falls within the parameters of the business case. The investment decision concerns whether the organization will commit to the construction/build phase of the project with the preferred tenderer, thereby incurring the cost and risk associated with the build phase. The investment decision itself should be based around predetermined criteria. Once the organization has agreed the evaluation process, the investment decision is concerned less with the outcome of that process than that the process was correctly followed. Once the investment decision has been made, final contract negotiations can be concluded and contracts signed.

Procurement: Summary of key decisions and key documentation

Key decision: the investment decision – will the organization proceed with the construction/build stage of the project and incur the cost and risk that that will entail?

Decision makers will be asking: does the response of the preferred tenderer meet the business case?

Key decision-making document: bid evaluation report (plus potentially the business case updated to reflect the response of the market, where the market response falls outside the parameters of the original business case.)
Other generic documentation may include expressions of interest and contract documentation.

Build

The build or construction stage commences after the investment decision is made to proceed with the project and completes at commissioning of the asset (or 'go live' in software development terms). At this point there will be a handover of the asset from the contractor to the operator unless the contract also incorporates operations.

The key decision-making documents are the contract and the project completion report, which, amongst other content associated with project completion and handover, addresses the lessons learned on the project. For the purposes of this book, the decisions made during the build stage of the project are relatively incidental. The decision making that characterized earlier stages in the project lifecycle related to key decisions regarding the ongoing development of the project. Once a project enters the build stage the key decision points for the project have been passed. Even the 'go live' decision is predominantly a technical one, with preceding decisions already determining the intention of the organization to go live once readiness for service is established.

Service delivery

Service delivery is the ongoing stage involving the asset entering operation in order to deliver services. This stage is sometimes referred to as benefits realization, although there is an argument that benefits are realized through the successful implementation of programmes of work rather than individual projects. Ideally, organizations should audit commissioned projects at various times throughout their life to determine the extent to which the benefits defined in the project or programme business case have been delivered.

Integration

Key documents and milestones

Having developed the project lifecycle, the key project documents discussed above that are used to support and inform the major project decisions can now be added to the diagram in Figure 8.1. Major milestones that the project achieves over the project lifecycle can also be added. These are the milestones that will be common to most if not all projects, and are those that will be of greatest interest to senior executives, since they reflect major decision points in the project and will be the subject of project board, strategic advisors group and investment decision group meetings. Figure 8.2 shows the project lifecycle and the key documents and major milestones integrated with it.

Managing estimates and costs

In the broadest sense, projects are in part defined by their estimated cost. This is particularly so for government projects where, driven by media interest, the estimated cost is even used as an adjective to describe the project – 'the $4 billion West Coast Highway'. The release of cost estimates by the project tends to set expectations both within the organization and externally. As estimates change over the course of the project as it gains greater definition, publicity is generated and since the change is often an increase, the publicity is not usually positive.

The underestimation of project costs has two main causes. First there is the problem of optimism bias whereby project estimators have an unduly positive outlook on the project in the early days of its development and neglect to account for the inevitable issues that will arise. The second problem is due to the competition between projects to gain funding and the expectation that a project with a lower capital cost is more likely to receive funding than a higher-cost competitor. Thus estimators may deliberately underestimate the likely outturn cost of the project in order to ensure it receives funding.

Even if these problems are eliminated, on average half of all projects will still be underestimated, thereby setting unrealistic expectations of the project's outturn cost. When successive estimates are revised upwards, the project is criticized for the 'escalating cost'. This issue can be particularly noticeable in the public service, where there can be a desire by politicians to announce projects at their inception with an associated estimate, combined with intense scrutiny by the media of the subsequent project. After sufficient criticism, projects become wary of releasing or even developing early estimates of project costs. This of course impacts the ability of treasury departments to forward plan capital programmes.

It therefore makes sense for executives involved in the governance of a project or programme to manage the release of information concerning the estimated cost of projects. The two issues to be addressed are therefore: 1) improving estimating policy and processes to overcome the tendency towards underestimation; and 2) managing expectations

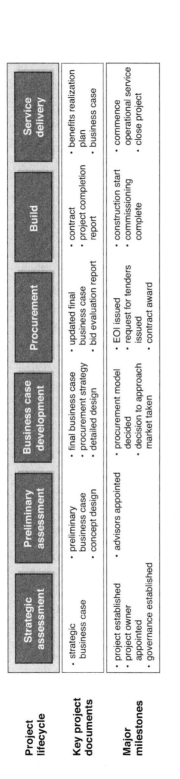

Project lifecycle	Strategic assessment	Preliminary assessment	Business case development	Procurement	Build	Service delivery
Key project documents	• strategic business case	• preliminary business case • concept design	• final business case • procurement strategy • detailed design	• updated final business case • bid evaluation report	• contract • project completion report	• benefits realization plan • business case
Major milestones	• project established • project owner appointed • governance established	• advisors appointed	• procurement model decided • decision to approach market taken	• EOI issued • request for tenders issued • contract award	• construction start • commissioning complete	• commence operational service • close project

Figure 8.2 Project lifecycle with key documents and major milestones added

both within and externally to the organization when releasing project estimates. Addressing 1) is outside the remit of this text; however, the second point can benefit from some relatively simple remedies that can be incorporated within an integrated project delivery framework.

An estimate can be produced at any point in a project's life. What varies is the accuracy that accompanies that estimate, with accuracy improving as the design is refined. Thus, whenever an estimate is released for a project, it should be accompanied by its associated accuracy and the basis upon which it has been developed. The other opportunity, again especially in relation to the public service, is the development of a standard terminology around the usage of the terms 'estimates' and 'costs' to avoid public and media confusion. For example, if an initial estimate for a project is $250 million and a subsequent, more accurate estimate based upon more detailed design and investigations indicates a new estimate of $350 million, this does not constitute a 'cost blow-out' as the media has been known to portray such issues. At this point in the project's development, ahead of the build phase, no significant cost has been incurred, whereas the implication is that the public purse has been faced with a $100 million overspend. It's not possible to have a 'cost blow-out' if no cost as such has been incurred. In fact, until contracts are signed, the organization has made no decision to invest any money in the construction of the project.

One simple yet effective measure to avoid this confusion, or bad behaviour, on the part of the media is to carefully avoid use of the word 'costs' when in fact it is estimates that are being referred to. This approach begins to educate the media and public of the important difference between the two. While this educational process may be a long one, and the media may not always wish to be educated at the expense of a good headline, eventually it will result in a reframing of the public understanding of projects and their estimates and costs. The following provides an example of this approach, although every organization will wish to tailor it for their own needs.

Linking estimates, costs, accuracy and announcements

During the strategic assessment phase, the project is unlikely to have undertaken any design of sufficient rigor to properly allow an estimate for the project to be developed. At best, any estimate is probably top-down (ie not built up from design detail) and based upon recent similar projects, providing an accuracy perhaps of the order of ± 100 per cent. (Note: each organization will need to determine the degree of accuracy associated with the release of an estimate at the various points in the project lifecycle.). In the case of government, any announcement at this stage should be of the form 'WE are investigating various options for the development of [...]. A preliminary estimate for this project will be available in approximately [...] months.'

The preliminary assessment phase sees the development of a concept design that can form the basis of a preliminary estimate. This estimate may have an accuracy of the order of ± 50 per cent. The accompanying government announcement is of the form 'This is a preliminary estimate based upon a concept design. More detailed estimates will be developed before any investment decision is made.' Any press release necessarily mentions the accuracy level.

During business case development the final business case is completed, based upon a detailed design. This is the organization's best estimate ahead of seeking and receiving any response from the market. This pre-market estimate has now firmed to perhaps ± 15 per cent. The accompanying government announcement is of the form 'This is a pre-market estimate developed as part of the government's final business case for the project. The decision to proceed with the project will be subject to the market providing a value for money response to our request for tenders.'

At the completion of the procurement phase the organization has received a market price for the project – note the terminology, it is neither an estimate nor a cost. The market price, or contract price, represents a commitment from the successful tenderer to deliver the project for that amount and so the likely outturn cost can be expressed at this point as 'contract price plus variations'. (The terminology can be adjusted to account for different procurement models, such as alliances where the market price may be referred to as a target cost estimate.) The accompanying government announcement is of the form '[company name] has committed to deliver the project at a price of [contract price], which represents a value for money outcome in line with the government's business case.'

Note that to this point there has been no mention of the term 'cost' on the grounds that only the relatively minor costs associated with the development of the design and business case have been incurred. The main costs on the project are incurred during the build phase and so it can reasonably be argued that a true 'cost blow-out' can only occur when the out-turn cost significantly exceeds the contract price. And at this point criticism is probably warranted.

This careful use of terminology accompanied by caveats on the accuracy of the various estimates will, over time, increase the public's understanding of the project development process. Concurrently, while the media will not always respond in accordance with the logic of this approach, it will become more apparent when the headlines are sensationalist rather than accurate. When this occurs, politicians will also be better placed to defend the government and the project against unwarranted media attack.

The various estimates/costs, their accuracies and the announcements that accompany them have been added to the project lifecycle diagram shown in Figure 8.3.

Project approvals

All organizations will benefit from a consistent position on the main approvals over the life of the project. These approvals focus on the main 'go/no go' decisions made in relation to the project and, being for the main part financially focused, will usually be made by the investment decision group. They are based on information received from the project board plus the key project documents. Again, each organization will wish to tailor these approvals to meet their own needs, although it seems likely that the following represents the minimum number of decision points.

- At the completion of the strategic assessment phase, the project board (or perhaps the programme board) will decide if the project supports the strategic objectives of the organization and therefore should proceed. The decision is based upon the strategic business case.
- Upon completion of the preliminary assessment, the investment decision group approves funding for the development of the final business case. This decision is based on the preliminary business case. At this point the investment decision group has made an 'in principle' commitment to the project, providing it can be shown to represent value for money.
- At the end of the business case development phase, the project board approves the final business case, which the investment decision group will use to determine if the project is likely to

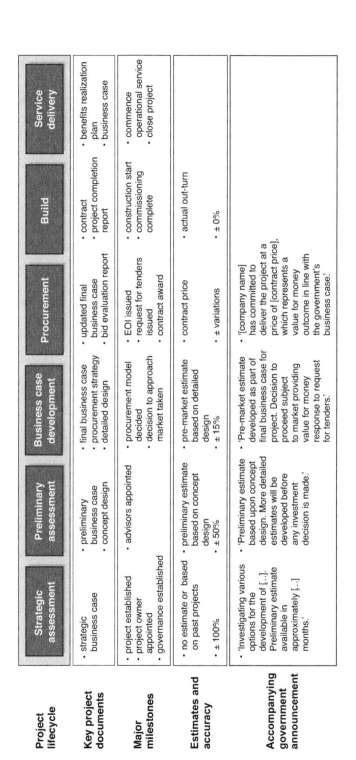

Project lifecycle	Strategic assessment	Preliminary assessment	Business case development	Procurement	Build	Service delivery
Key project documents	• strategic business case	• preliminary business case • concept design	• final business case • procurement strategy • detailed design	• updated final business case • bid evaluation report	• contract • project completion report	• benefits realization plan • business case
Major milestones	• project established • project owner appointed • governance established	• advisors appointed	• procurement model decided • decision to approach market taken	• EOI issued • request for tenders issued • contract award	• construction start • commissioning complete	• commence operational service • close project
Estimates and accuracy	• no estimate or based on past projects • ± 100%	• preliminary estimate based on concept design ± 50%	• pre-market estimate based on detailed design ± 15%	• contract price • ± variations	• actual out-turn • ± 0%	
Accompanying government announcement	• 'Investigating various options for the development of [...]. Preliminary estimate available in approximately [...] months.'	• 'Preliminary estimate based upon concept design. More detailed estimates will be developed before any investment decision is made.'	• 'Pre-market estimate developed as part of final business case for project. Decision to proceed subject to market providing value for money response to request for tenders.'	• '[company name] has committed to deliver the project at a price of [contract price], which represents a value for money outcome in line with the government's business case.'		

Figure 8.3 Project lifecycle with integrated estimates and government announcements

provide value for money. At this point, the investment decision group approves the commitment to fund the project and approves the procurement model.

● At the end of the procurement phase, the investment decision group approves the investment decision based upon the final business case, updated to reflect the market price. This approval allows the signing of the build or construction contract(s).

Common modifications to the above include combining the approvals associated with the strategic and preliminary business cases (ie having only the one approval) and including an additional approval during the procurement phase for the issuing of tenders. The above approvals are added to the project lifecycle diagram in Figure 8.4. Subsequent approvals occurring later in the project lifecycle such as readiness for service, project closure, etc. are made by the project board and are secondary decisions associated with an already-committed project. As such they do not constitute 'go/no go' project decisions, so have not been incorporated within this strategic framework.

Staged gates

Project owners and other decision makers require confidence that their projects are well placed for success. A level of confidence is achieved through their involvement in the project governance arrangements and this confidence will be enhanced through the application of good process such as project management methodologies and an integrated project delivery framework. Staged gates are a further project assurance process that involves a project 'passing through' a gate designed to test its suitability to proceed to the next stage of its development. This is a step beyond the approval process discussed above, where those making the investment decision question the project regarding its suitability to proceed. Instead it seeks to provide those decision makers with additional assurance before they make their decision.

The PRINCE methodology (OGC, 2005a) introduced the concept of defining a project as a series of separate stages, albeit with overlaps. Each stage completes with an end of stage assessment to ensure that the stage had indeed delivered what was planned and that the project is well placed to proceed to the next stage. The project owner can therefore gain assurance stage by stage that the project is progressing according to plan.

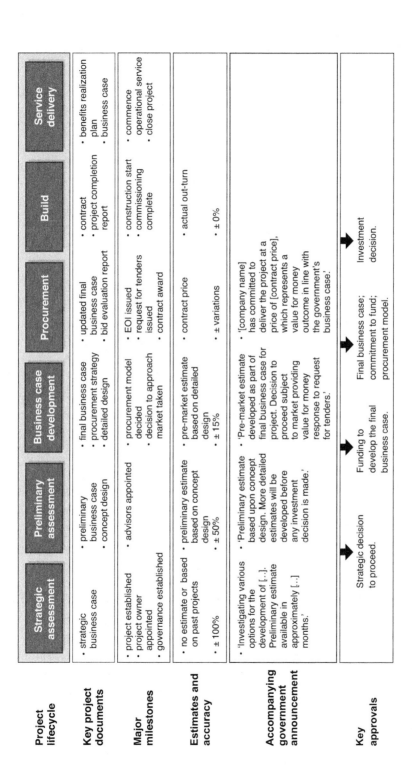

Project lifecycle	Strategic assessment	Preliminary assessment	Business case development	Procurement	Build	Service delivery
Key project documents	• strategic business case	• preliminary business case • concept design	• final business case • procurement strategy • detailed design	• updated final business case • bid evaluation report	• contract • project completion report	• benefits realization plan • business case
Major milestones	• project established • project owner appointed • governance established	• advisors appointed	• procurement model decided • decision to approach market taken	• EOI issued • request for tenders issued • contract award	• construction start • commissioning complete	• commence operational service • close project
Estimates and accuracy	• no estimate or based on past projects • ± 100%	• preliminary estimate based on concept design • ± 50%	• pre-market estimate based on detailed design • ± 15%	• contract price • ± variations	• actual out-turn • ± 0%	
Accompanying government announcement	• 'Investigating various options for the development of [...]. Preliminary estimate available in approximately [...] months.'	• 'Preliminary estimate based upon concept design. More detailed estimates will be developed before any investment decision is made.'	• 'Pre-market estimate developed as part of final business case for project. Decision to proceed subject to market providing value for money response to request for tenders.'	• '[company name] has committed to deliver the project at a price of [contract price], which represents a value for money outcome in line with the government's business case.'		
Key approvals	Strategic decision to proceed.	Funding to develop the final business case.	Final business case; commitment to fund; procurement model.	Investment decision.		

Figure 8.4 Project lifecycle with key approvals integrated

In government project delivery, this approach has been taken a step further with the introduction of the Gateway Process (OGC, undated c) developed by the UK Government around 2000. This process consists of project reviews by a small team of experts independent of the project. These reviews take place at five gates, with an additional review at the programme level. The gates are shown in Table 8.1.

A Gateway Review involves the review of project documentation and, importantly, interviews with all key project stakeholders including the project owner, key members of the project team and stakeholders external to the project (and perhaps the organization). It culminates in a short report presented to the project owner on the final day of the review. The review itself is completed in around four days or less, although there is some preparation involved.

Reviews are timed to occur ahead of the key decision points on the project so that when issues or risks are identified, the project has time to

Table 8.1 The five gates of the UK Government's gateway process

Gate	Gate Name	Purpose
0	Strategic Assessment	Programme level review that investigates the strategy, direction, planning and benefits of the programme and its constituent projects. This review is repeatable throughout the life of the programme.
I	Business justification	Project review focusing on ensuring clarity around benefits, strategic fit, objectives and the initial cost–benefit tradeoff.
2	Delivery strategy	Project review of the updated business case and the proposed procurement model.
3	Investment decision	Project review of the final business case and tender evaluation report ahead of appointing the delivery partner.
4	Readiness for service	Project review that investigates the readiness of the organization to transition from the project environment to the operational environment.
5	Operational review and benefits realization	This review confirms that the planned benefits are being delivered and that the service is meeting performance expectations. It is repeatable.

rectify or mitigate them. The Gateway Process can deliver considerable benefits, including:

- reduced time and budget overruns on projects;
- improved alignment of initiatives with government strategic objectives;
- an increase in the investment confidence of the investment decision group.

The Gateway Process is proving increasingly popular amongst governments worldwide and is a worthwhile addition to an integrated project delivery framework. The review gates have been added to the project lifecycle diagram in Figure 8.5. Note that they occur ahead of the key approvals to ensure the project has sufficient time to address any issues or risks identified by the review ahead of the approval. The programme level gate, gate 0, is not shown since it occurs outside of the project environment.

The integrated project delivery framework

Figure 8.5 displays the complete integrated project delivery framework. Clearly any organization can adapt the model to suit its purpose, making it more or less detailed. Remember that the objective of the model is to apply a degree of high-level consistency to project delivery within an organization at an overarching level. In this manner it benefits both project decision makers and those engaged in the minutiae of project delivery.

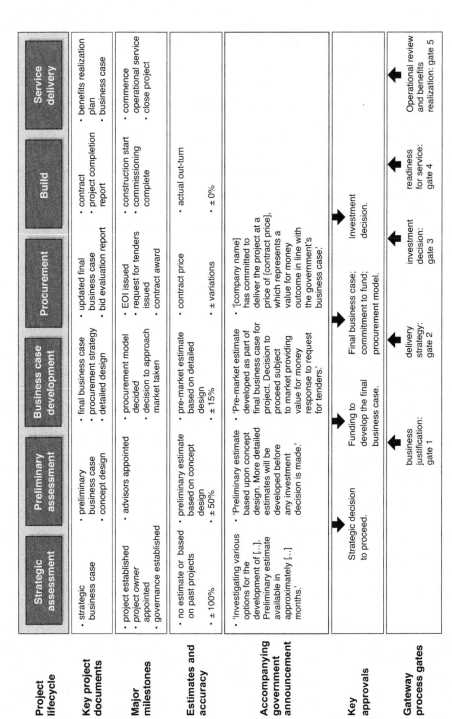

Figure 8.5 An integrated project delivery framework

Appendix I:
Example project
governance policy

The following is an example of a project governance policy that can readily be modified to meet the needs of most organizations.

Overview

This policy addresses the project governance arrangements for all projects undertaken by [*insert organization's name*]. Its primary focus is high-risk projects as determined by [*the organization should have criteria or possibly a high-level project risk assessment model that determines the risk level of any particular project*] and the governance framework is designed to support such projects. The policy also addresses lower-risk projects by enabling flexible governance arrangements.

Applicability

This policy is applicable to all projects. Projects that are therefore covered by this policy include [*select as appropriate for the organization: asset and non-asset solutions, change management projects and ICT and policy projects*]. It shall be adhered to by all employees, as well as by consultants and contractors working for the organization. This policy is not applicable to non-capital or operational activities. It is not applicable to projects that are currently (at the time of approval of this document) being implemented or constructed.

Definitions

[*Add other definitions as necessary. Any role or body that appears in the framework will need to be defined.*]

Accountable   Accountable means answerable to your superior.

Investment decision group   [*This group normally already exists within an organization and often does not need to be separately constituted. It may be known as a budget committee.*] The investment decision group makes the major investment decisions on a project.

Key project documentation   The key project documentation is: [*adjust to suit, naming conventions and needs of the organization. Each organization should identify a family of documents that must be produced for each project undertaken. If not, then individual project boards should identify these documents. Refer to chapter 8.*]

- strategic business case;
- preliminary business case ;
- final business case;
- procurement strategy;
- project completion report.
- [*Add other documentation as necessary.*]

Project   A project is an undertaking of fixed duration created to deliver a new, enhanced or modified service for the organization.

Project board   The project board is the committee responsible for directing the project. Each project must have a project board, although a number of smaller projects could come under the umbrella of a single project board. The core members of the project board are the project owner, senior supplier, senior user and project director. Others may be invited to attend by the project owner.

Project director   The person who manages the project owner's interests in the project on a day-to-day basis.

Project manager   The nominated person who leads the project team and is assigned the authority and responsibility for managing the project within the constraints of scope, budget, schedule and quality as defined by the project owner.

Project owner   The person accountable for the success of the project and the chair of the project board.

Senior user   The person(s) who represents the interests and viewpoint of users on the project board and supports the project owner in directing the project.

Senior supplier   The person(s) who represents the interests and viewpoint of suppliers on the project board and supports the project owner in directing the project.

Strategic advisors' group   A group comprised of senior advisors whose role is to provide advice and support to the project owner and project board and to monitor and report on the alignment of the project with their organization's needs.

Stakeholder working group   A group comprised of technical advisors whose role is to provide advice and support to the project manager and project team on technical matters that have an impact on their own organizations.

Project governance framework for high-risk projects

[*Organization's name*] will manage high-risk projects in accordance with the following framework. Further detail on the operation of the project governance framework and policy is contained within the project governance procedure [*a document that provides greater detail around the operation of the project governance arrangements*]. The project governance structure shall generally be in accordance with that shown in Figure A1.1.

Role of the project board

All high-risk projects shall have a dedicated project board that shall operate in accordance with this framework. The project board is chaired by the project owner and should ideally contain no more than six people, to maintain decision-making efficiency.

The project board is responsible for directing the project. In discharging this responsibility it will approve the key project documentation and work to resolve issues escalated by the project manager and project director.

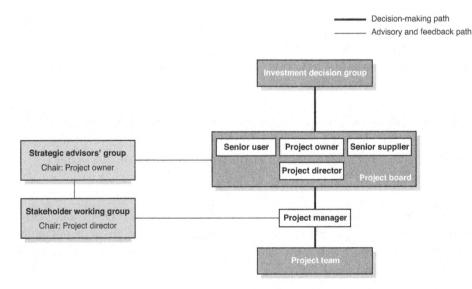

Figure A1.1   The project governance structure

Role of the investment decision group

The investment decision group has the following responsibilities:

- approve funding of the development of a final business case for the project;
- approve funding of the project in accordance with the funding requirements of the final business case;
- approve major variations to funding;
- address and resolve issues raised by the project board;
- address and resolve matters of policy raised by the project board.

Role of strategic advisors' group

The strategic advisors' group represents key stakeholders who have a valid interest in the project. It is chaired by the project owner. The strategic advisors group has the following responsibilities:

- review and provide input to project documentation;
- provide advice to the project owner;
- raise issues that have an impact on their organization's involvement in the project;
- keep their host organizations or departments appraised of project developments.

Role of stakeholder working group

The stakeholder working group represents the interests of stakeholders operating at the technical level. It is chaired by the project director or project manager. The stakeholder working group is responsible for monitoring project technical developments to ensure they remain consistent with their own organization's or department's requirements.

Roles and responsibilities within the project governance framework

Project owner

The project owner is the person accountable for the success of the project and owns the service whose delivery the project will facilitate and the project business case. All projects, irrespective of their assigned risk level, shall have a single nominated project owner. The project owner has the following responsibilities:

- determines the composition of and chairs the project board;
- chairs the strategic advisors' group;
- owns the project budget;
- appoints the project director;
- provides direction to the project director and project manager.

Project director

The project director supports the project owner and ensures the project owner's business needs are being met. The responsibilities and delegations of the project director are determined by the project owner but will normally encompass the following:

- chairing of the stakeholder working group;
- assisting in establishment of the project team;
- assisting the project owner in stakeholder management;
- acting as the main point of contact between the project manager and [*insert organization's name*];
- establishing client reporting arrangements;
- managing business resources.

Senior supplier

The senior supplier is a senior representative of the project's suppliers and provides their perspective and expertise. The senior supplier is responsible for:

- ensuring the necessary supplier resources are committed to the project;
- advising and informing the project board of supplier issues;
- ensuring the quality of outputs and products provided by suppliers.

Senior user

The senior user represents the end users of the delivered service and promotes their concerns and interests. The senior user is responsible for:

- representing the interests of users;
- establishing and chairing user groups where required;
- negotiating and developing user requirements and other user documentation;
- identifying and committing user resources for the project.

Project manager

The project manager is accountable to the project owner for managing the delivery of the project within the constraints of scope, budget, schedule and quality that are defined by the project owner. The project manager is responsible for:

- planning and managing the necessary activities to enable the project to be delivered within the above constraints;
- appointing project team members and is supported in this by the project owner and project director.

Project governance framework for medium-risk and low-risk projects

This section describes project governance arrangements for medium- and low-risk projects.

All projects are required to have a single nominated project owner. All projects must have a project board; however, a single project board can encompass more than one project. In such cases the membership of the project board must reflect the needs of the project and, in particular, the project owner must be chosen on the basis of representing the business or service needs that the project will deliver. The need for a project board, and whether that project board is dedicated to that project, is determined by the project owner. A single project director may act as such for a number of projects. On medium-risk and low-risk projects there may be no need for a project director and the project owner may also fulfil the role of project manager and/or senior user. The decision on combining project governance roles is made by the project owner.

The need for the strategic advisors' group and stakeholder working group is dependent upon the number of stakeholders and the complexity of stakeholder relationships. Only quite complex projects are likely to have the need for a stakeholder working group. Smaller projects with fewer stakeholders may not require a stakeholder advisory group for the management of stakeholder needs where the project owner can fulfil that role on an ad hoc basis.

Policy approval

This policy was approved by [*insert name of approving body*] on [*date*] and becomes official policy on [*date*].

Policy owner

[*Insert name and position of the owner of the policy. The policy owner will normally be a corporate level group or perhaps a programme office if such an office sits across all projects in the organization.*]

Related policy and procedures

The following policies and procedures are related to this policy:

- [*Add as required.*]

Appendix II:
Terms of reference and modus operandi of project governance bodies

The following provides high-level terms of reference and modus operandi for the various bodies that make up the project governance model. These may prove useful as a basis for organizations developing their own project governance framework.

Project board

Establishment

The project board is the key decision-making body on the project and is established at the commencement of the project. Members are appointed by the project owner, possibly with the assistance of programme management.

Membership

The members of the project board are:

Project owner: The project owner is accountable for the success of the project and chairs the project board. The project owner is the owner of the business service, the delivery of which will be facilitated by that project. The project owner owns the business case and has project budget responsibility.

Senior user: The senior user represents the interests of business, operational and maintenance users. This role is responsible for the definition of user requirements and for ensuring the project delivers to those requirements. The senior user role may also represent senior managers who have a major interest in the project and whose activities will be affected by the project. If there are multiple sources of funding for the project, a representative of a major funding body may fulfil this role.

Senior supplier: The senior supplier represents the interests of those supplying services to the project and is primarily responsible for the delivery of the project's assets. The holder of this role may change as the project moves from the business case phase to the construction phase.

Project director: The project director is accountable to the project owner for ensuring the project owner's needs are met. This role undertakes day-to-day management and makes decisions on behalf of the project owner.

Size of the project board

- Although there are four roles on the project board, certain roles may be shared or combined.
- The project owner role cannot be shared because accountability for the success of the project cannot be split.
- The project director role should not be shared or split on a major project.

- There may be more than one senior user, although it is recommended there be no more than two.
- There may be more than one senior supplier, especially when there are both internal and external suppliers or providers involved in the project. It is recommended there be no more than two.
- Business representatives should always be in the majority on the project board to ensure a service delivery focus is maintained.
- The project manager is not a member of the project board but reports into it.
- Experts can be invited to attend project board meetings; however, their input is normally obtained through the strategic advisors group or the stakeholder working group.
- Once the project board exceeds around six persons, decision making becomes less effective.

All project board members should attend all project board meetings.

Decision making

- The project owner is the chair of the project board and appoints project board members.
- The project owner is accountable for the success of the project and so all project board decisions require the support of the project owner.

The project board shall:

- approve the terms of reference of the project board;
- approve the responsibilities of project board members;
- support the project owner;
- work with key stakeholders to meet their needs and ensure their issues are addressed at the project board;
- approve the appointment of the project manager;
- provide direction to the project manager;
- approve the responsibilities of the project manager;
- approve the project structure as developed by the project manager;
- approve reporting and communication arrangements;
- approve project documentation, which may include:
  - the project business case (and material changes to it);
  - the project management plan;

- feasibility studies;
- concept designs;
- output specifications;
- options analyses;
- the procurement strategy;
- the project completion report and lessons learned.
- ensure project stakeholder engagement is being adequately addressed;
- confirm the project's operating parameters and tolerances with programme management, including budget and schedule tolerances for project stages and for the project as a whole;
- address and resolve project issues escalated by the project director or project manager;
- escalate issues that cannot be resolved to the investment decision group;
- approve any material changes to scope, budget, schedule or quality;
- ratify critical design decisions.

Meetings of the project board

The project board should be convened at the commencement of the project (i.e. during the strategic assessment) and continue meeting until the project completion report has been delivered. The frequency of project board meetings should be appropriate to the scale and complexity of the project and is dependent to a large extent on the issues to be addressed. In certain circumstances the project board may need to meet weekly, but at less critical points in the project's lifecycle monthly meetings may be sufficient. If a project board meets too infrequently it runs the risk of becoming too remote from the project.

Record keeping

The project board provides direction to the project. Its decisions therefore need to be clear and unambiguous. On a long project it is possible that one or more project board roles could change hands over the duration and therefore it is important that the status of any document issued to the project board for approval is understood. This avoids revisiting decisions. Project board members can also use 'under-studies' to ensure another member of their staff is kept appraised of the project and the decisions reached so that in the event the project board member moves from their position, continuity can be maintained until a new board member is chosen and briefed by the understudy.

When a project document is presented for approval, the project board decision should be one of the following:

- approved;
- approved subject to [list the changes that must be made for the document to be considered approved];
- not approved – rework required in the following areas: [list].

A similar approach is beneficial for issues that have been addressed by the project board. Issues need to be logged and the outcome reached by the project board on each issue recorded. Issue resolution normally takes one of the following forms:

- the issue is resolved and the outcome recorded;
- further information is requested of the project manager or project director to assist in resolving the issue;
- the project board considers the issue is a matter for resolution by the project manager and requests the project manager to advise;
- the issue is unable to be resolved by the project board and is escalated to the investment decision group for resolution;
- the issue is taken off-line by a project board member.

Investment decision group

Membership

The investment decision group is normally a pre-existing committee within an organization. It may be referred to as the budget committee, budget review committee, expenditure (review) committee, etc. As such its membership is normally predetermined.

Terms of reference

The investment decision group will:

- approve, or otherwise, funding the development of a final business case for the project based upon the information contained within the preliminary business case and the presentation and information provided by the project owner;
- approve, or otherwise, funding to complete the project based upon information contained within the final business case and the presentation and information provided by the project owner;
- approve, or otherwise, material variations to funding based upon an updated final business case and representation from the project owner and/or project director;
- stop projects from proceeding at preliminary business case stage where the preliminary business case describes a project that is not aligned with the organization's goals;
- stop projects from proceeding at business case stage if the business case is not considered viable, affordable or value for money;
- refer the preliminary business case back to the project board for reworking where it does not meet the organization's requirements for such a document or where further information or analysis is required. [Note: the investment decision group's secretariat will often act as a filter to ensure the quality of documentation provided to the investment decision group is adequate; however, this does presuppose the necessary level of understanding and sophistication in respect of projects within the secretariat.];
- address and resolve issues raised by the project board;
- address and resolve matters of policy raised by the project board (note: if there is a strong programme management board, it may address escalated issues and matters of policy);
- forward approved preliminary business cases to [financial planning function] for inclusion in forward budget programmes.

Strategic advisors' group

The strategic advisors' group shall undertake its activities as follows:

- the strategic advisors' group is chaired by the project owner;
- strategic advisors' group members must have the authority to make decisions on behalf of their organizations. Decisions made by

strategic advisors' group members are taken to represent the views of their respective organizations;

- members are to work with an alternate so that in the event of their absence from a meeting, their views can be represented by someone with equivalent authority and understanding of the project and its issues.

Members of the strategic advisors' group have the following responsibilities:

- review project documentation and advise the chair of any issues or concerns they have with it;
- identify issues and risks that may impact the project;
- raise any issues members have with the project within the strategic advisors' group initially;
- provide advice on project issues. In particular, provide detailed advice on areas relating to their organization's specific interest in the project;
- work as a group to provide the project owner with a single agreed position on project issues (wherever possible);
- disseminate non-confidential information regarding the project within members' host organizations;
- where a stakeholder working group has been established, nominate one or more officers from their organization to sit on that group and provide the technical advice required;
- support the project owner.

Stakeholder working group

The stakeholder working group is chaired by the project director. The project owner or project manager may chair the group in the absence of the project director.

Members have the following responsibilities:

- represent the interests of their organizations;
- keep their representative on the strategic advisors' group appraised of developments and decisions taken by the stakeholder working group;
- work with an alternate so that in the event of their absence at a meeting their views can be represented by someone with equivalent authority and understanding of the project and its issues;

- review project documentation and advise the chair of any issues or concerns they have with it;
- identify issues and risks that may have an impact on the project;
- raise any issues members have with the project within the stakeholder working group initially;
- provide advice on project issues and in particular, provide detailed advice on areas relating to their organization's specific interest in the project;
- work as a group to provide the project director with a single agreed position on project issues (wherever possible);
- disseminate non-confidential information regarding the project within members host organizations;
- support the project owner, project director and project manager.

Appendix III: Role descriptions

The following role descriptions cover each project board member as well as the project manager's role in respect of the project governance arrangements. They may prove of use to an organization either developing a project governance framework or structuring the governance of a particular project.

Project owner

Introduction

The project owner is accountable for the success of the project. They are the owner of the project and must have responsibility for the project's budget.

The project owner is drawn from the business itself. The more important the project, the higher the position the project owner holds in the organization. As a result of their business focus, the project owner views the project as a means to an end – the end being the benefits that the project is designed to deliver. They own these benefits and the outcomes that the project will deliver and their ownership of the project is focused on ensuring these benefits are delivered to the business. Ownership of the project confers ownership of the documentation that defines the project, in particular the business case. The project owner role on any project should not be outsourced and should be considered a core part of the business of the organization.

A project can have only one project owner – the role cannot be split, since accountability itself cannot be split. In the event of multiple sources of funding for a project, a single project owner should be chosen with other funding parties being represented in other roles on the project board, such as senior user.

Major responsibilities

Note that if the project does not have a project director, the project owner's responsibilities will need to encompass those of a project director.

Establish the project's governance arrangements

- Drive the initiation of the project upon appointment;
- establish the project board and select project board members based on the project's needs;
- recruit the project director;
- establish the strategic advisors' group and stakeholder working group;
- work with the project director to identify the project manager and source project advisors;
- ensure all stakeholders understand the operation of the project governance arrangements and their role in it.

Be the primary sponsor of the project

- Present themselves as the main face of the project, both internally and external to the organization;
- manage stakeholders with the assistance of the project director and ensure stakeholders needs are met and their issues are addressed;
- ensure ongoing stakeholder support for the project;
- ensure stakeholders are aligned with the project's objectives and that they remain so throughout the project;
- manage upwards rather than downwards – downwards management from the customer's perspective is the role of the project director.

Note that on smaller projects where a project director is not engaged, the project owner will have to manage downwards.

Ensure the project maintains a service delivery focus

- Ensure the overall project focus is on delivering services rather than just the asset;
- ensure project costing, budget and cost controls are focused on whole-of-life costs rather than only capital cost;
- ensure the project benefits are clearly stated and that a clear plan is developed for realizing those benefits;
- ensure the overall output specification is designed around delivery of benefits;
- develop the definition of the project from the owner's perspective, ensuring clear articulation of the project's benefits, objectives, drivers and critical success factors;
- ensure the project focuses on benefits realization throughout its life;
- ensure the project is aligned with the goals and vision of the organization.

Monitor and control progress

- Drive the project forward and ensure that momentum and progress is maintained;
- own and manage the project budget;
- where additional funds are required, present or support the case for such funds;
- own and manage the project business case and other key project documentation such as the project plan, preliminary business case or equivalent, etc;
- ensure project documentation is reviewed by the project board and that documents are either approved or the necessary modifications required to achieve approval are articulated;
- approve major scope changes and ensure the business case reflects such changes.

Focus on the main risks and issues

- Ensure adequate attention is focused on risks and risk mitigation;
- where appropriate, ensure risk mitigation is adequately costed;

- resolve issues that have been escalated by the project manager and work with stakeholders where necessary to address such issues;
- where necessary, seek independent advice on the project.

Resource the project for success

- Ensure adequate project owner resources are allocated to the project to assist in defining service delivery outcomes, desired benefits, output specification, etc;
- ensure sufficient user resources are deployed on the project for the production of user specifications, acceptance criteria, etc;
- ensure external supplier resources are adequate in terms of numbers, skills and expertise;
- ensure they allocate adequate of their own time to the project.

Maintain a strategic perspective on the project

- Liaise with the programme management office (if extant) regarding resourcing, quality criteria and the positioning of the project as part of the greater programme;
- understand the strategic objectives of the organization and ensure the project remains aligned with those objectives throughout its life;
- maintain awareness of any broader environmental (not just green) considerations and how the project has an impact on or could be affected by such considerations.

Specific responsibilities

The project owner is responsible for:

- appointing project board members;
- appointing the project director and agreeing their remit and delegated authority;
- chairing the project board;
- chairing the strategic advisors group;
- agreeing all major plans and any deviations from them;
- approving the full business case and recommending it to the investment decision group;
- approving major project deliverables;

- communicating information about the project to the organization and stakeholder groups as necessary;
- resolving conflicts escalated by the project team, client or supplier, or escalating these issues to the investment decision group;
- resolving conflicts between project team, end users and suppliers, or escalating as necessary;
- agreeing the project tolerances for time, quality and cost (with the programme management office if applicable);
- providing overall strategic guidance for the project;
- addressing the risk(s) associated with the project;
- ensuring project quality assurance is adequate and consistent with the organization's norm (possibly as defined by the programme management office);
- providing advice and direction to the project director and project manager as required;
- closing the project;
- approving the end of project report and the lessons learned report.

Ideal characteristics and skills

When selecting a project owner, the primary consideration is the person's position within the organization and whether that position owns the service delivery outcomes the project will deliver. The person identified via this route may not exhibit all the characteristics and skills listed below; however, this is a secondary consideration that perhaps can be addressed in part by further support for the project owner, training or the appointment of a project director with the necessary skills:

- seniority commensurate with the scale of the project;
- decisive, involved and not just a figurehead;
- prepared to accept accountability and responsibility for the project;
- reasonable understanding of projects and the project lifecycle;
- good communication skills;
- strong understanding of the business case and its development process;
- detailed knowledge of business issues and desired business outcomes;
- in the event the project's business case does not provide value for money, be prepared to report same to senior management and, if necessary, terminate the project;

- able to focus on the big picture and understand the project in the context of the overall programme;
- be a good negotiator who is able to reconcile the disparate needs and drivers of users, suppliers and the business;
- recognize when the project is in difficulty and be prepared to act to resolve the issue;
- act in an open an honest manner in regard to the project;
- provide senior management and programme management with an honest appraisal of the project's progress.

Project director

Introduction

The project director is tasked with guarding the interests of the project owner when the project owner does not have the necessary time to devote to the project. The project director reports directly to the project owner and the project manager reports to the project director. In this respect, the project director provides the interface between project ownership and delivery.

The project director represents the customer and acts as the main point of contact with the project manager for the day-to-day management of the customer's interests. This role is responsible for ensuring the project objectives are delivered. For this to happen, the project director must ensure the project maintains a service delivery focus and will work with the project owner and project manager to ensure this is the case.

The person in this role must have adequate knowledge and information about the business to make informed decisions and must also have a detailed understanding of project management to appreciate the perspective of the project manager and project team. On large and complex projects, this is a difficult combination to achieve because those with sufficient understanding of the business are not always project specialists. Thus it is not always possible to source project directors from the business and it may be necessary to outsource this role. If the person is outsourced they will need to develop a good understanding of the business, work closely with business experts and integrate them into the project. The alternative approach of taking a business expert and training them in project delivery skills is unlikely to be effective on large and complex projects.

If the project director is seconded from the delivery side of the organization, the contractual arrangements and personal performance arrangements must all sit with the project owner, else there will inevitably be conflicts of interests.

Major responsibilities

Protect project owner's interests

- Provide project drive and momentum;
- maintain a service delivery perspective and a focus on business outcomes;
- keep project owner informed of issues and risks;
- monitor project progress against plans and review project manager's reports;
- monitor project expenditure against budget;
- monitor project quality;
- define protocols for control and management of the project;
- identify and select project advisors.

Assist project owner in management of stakeholders

- Support project owner in managing strategic advisors' group;
- manage the stakeholder working group, working with the project manager;
- balance the competing demands of the business, users and suppliers;
- ensure communications protocols are in place and effective in enabling sufficient dialogue to ensure ongoing alignment of stakeholders, contractors, end users and business resources.

Manage business resources

- Manage those resources providing business input to the project;
- ensure business inputs are provided with adequate levels of quality and detail and are timely;
- establish project team arrangements and work to foster teamwork.

Work with the project manager

- Develop project reporting and communications protocols;
- work with the project manager in the development of key project documentation and review all documents that proceed to the project board;
- keep project owner appraised of project activity;
- work with the project manager to resolve issues and escalate those that cannot be resolved;
- assist in the identification of risks and ensure mitigation strategies that meet business needs are developed;
- assist in coordinating and fostering teamwork.

Ideal characteristics and skills

- Decisive, with good clarity of purpose;
- good negotiator;
- ideally should have leadership qualities, with the ability to form a team around themselves;
- project management skills, possibly someone who has delivered large projects themselves in the past;
- detailed understanding of the department's business;
- detailed knowledge of the project's objectives, drivers, desired benefits, etc;
- understanding of procurement models and their suitability for different project types;
- knowledge of risk analysis and risk management;
- detailed knowledge of all elements of the project lifecycle;
- strong understanding of quality management principles and processes.

Senior user

The senior user represents those who will use the final product or service that the project delivers. This usage may comprise direct usage, indirect usage such as network operations where the product or asset forms part of the network, or even maintenance or facilities management where such considerations have a significant impact on the development of the project.

The role can also represent those whom the project may significantly affect. In particular, if the project has more than one source of funding, the project owner is normally chosen as a representative of the main funding organization and a senior user role could be used to provide a seat at the project board for the second funding organization. The senior user has the following responsibilities:

- support the project owner and assist them in directing the project;
- advise the project owner of any user issues that may have an impact on the project;
- advise the project owner of the impact on users of any changes being considered by the project board;
- assist the project owner as required in discussions with the strategic advisors' group on matters relating to user needs;
- negotiate with the project owner and senior supplier regarding the provision of user requirements balanced against the cost of providing those requirements;
- if there is more than one senior user, liaise closely with the other role holder for the benefit of the project;
- ensure all users are advised of any issues raised at the project board that may affect them;
- represent the interests of their user clients to the project;
- resolve conflicts between users on the project;
- provide the perspectives of all users on the matters the project board addresses;
- establish and chair user groups as necessary and ensure a consolidated user view is presented to the project board;
- maintain a focus on the delivery of users' needs throughout the project;
- take responsibility for the development of user requirements specifications, acceptance criteria and user acceptance testing documentation, aided as necessary by the project director and project manager;
- in developing user requirements, maintain a whole-of-life perspective;
- ensure the quality of user project deliverables meets the standards laid down by the project or programme management;
- commit resources to the project as required to meet the project needs and develop user documentation;
- assist the project manager in managing user resources on the project.

Senior supplier

The senior supplier represents the suppliers of services to the project and provides their perspective and expertise. The senior supplier has the following responsibilities:

- support the project owner and assist them in directing the project;
- advise the project owner of any supplier side issues that may have an impact on the project;
- ensure all suppliers are advised of any issues raised by the project board that may affect them;
- advise the project owner of the impact on suppliers of any changes being considered by the project board;
- represent the interests of all suppliers to the project;
- where supplier contracts are with the project owner's organization, work with the project owner to manage the activities of these suppliers and represent their interests and perspectives at the project board where these interests are not represented by a second senior supplier role;
- resolve conflicts between the suppliers to the project;
- provide the perspectives of all suppliers on the matters the project board addresses;
- chair supplier forums as necessary;
- interpret technical aspects of the project for the benefit of less technical project board members;
- assist the project owner as required in discussions with the strategic advisors' group on matters of a technical nature;
- if there is more than one senior supplier, liaise closely with the other role holder for the benefit of the project;
- commit resources to the project as required to meet the project needs;
- ensure the quality of those project deliverables that are the responsibility of suppliers meets the standards laid down by the project or programme management;
- relinquish the role of senior supplier in the event that the project has progressed in its lifecycle to a point where another organization is better placed to provide a person to fill the role.

Project manager

There are sufficient texts covering the role of the project manager for this book not to dwell further upon it. The following, then, covers that role only from the perspective of this project governance framework. The responsibilities of the project manager in relation to this project governance framework include:

- manage the delivery of the project on a day-to-day basis in accordance with the constraints established by the project owner and project board;
- liaise closely with the project director;
- work with and support the project director in managing the needs of stakeholders;
- provide project progress reports to the project director (there may be a reporting line also to the senior supplier);
- establish project control mechanisms in conjunction with the project director;
- establish communications protocols in conjunction with the project director;
- attend project board meetings as required and provide reports to the project board;
- support the project owner and project director in managing the activities of the strategic advisors' group and stakeholder working group;
- develop the project management structure of the project/project team;
- manage the integrated project team and, in particular, supplier resources on the project;
- manage the production of project documentation;
- ensure adequate project management methodologies are employed on the project and that these are consistent with organizational and programme management requirements.

References

Department of Treasury and Finance, Victorian Government (2007) *Gateway Lessons Learned*, [Online] <http://www.gatewayreview.dtf.vic. gov.au/CA256EF40083ACBF/WebObj/LessonsLearned/$File/Lessons% 20Learned.pdf>

Green, R and McDaniel, T (1998) *Competition in Electricity Supply: Will '1998' be worth it?* Power PWP-057. Working papers series of the Program on Workable Energy Regulation (POWER), a program of the University of California Energy Institute, California

Office of Urban Management, Queensland Government (2007) *South East Queensland Infrastructure Plan and Programme, 2007–2026*, Brisbane, Queensland Government

OGC (Office of Government Commerce) (2005a) *Managing Successful Projects with PRINCE2*, Norwich, The Stationery Office

OGC (2005b) *Common Causes of Project Failure*, [Online] Accessed April 2008. <http://www.ogc.gov.uk/documents/cp0015.pdf>

OGC (undated a) *Best Practice: Why IT projects fail*, [Online] Accessed April 2008. <http://www.ogc.gov.uk/documents/BPWhyITProjectsFail.pdf>

OGC (undated b) *Risk Potential Assessment*, [Online] Accessed April 2008. <http://www.ogc.gov.uk/documents/RiskPotentialAssessment.xls>

OGC (undated c) *OGC Gateway Review for Programmes and Projects*, [Online] Accessed April 2008. <http://www.ogc.gov.uk/what_is_ogc_ gateway_review.asp>

OGC (2007) *Managing Successful Programmes*, Norwich, The Stationery Office

Project Management Institute (2004) *A Guide to the Project Management Body of Knowledge* (PMBOK Guide), Third Edition, Newtown Square, PA, Project Management Institute

Queensland Department of Main Roads (2007) *Roads Implementation Program 2007–08 to 2011–12*, Brisbane, Queensland Government

Index

CPSIA information can be obtained
at www.ICGtesting.com
Printed in the USA
LVOW04*1054170416

483806LV00029BC/307/P